Praise for Lewis Grizzard!

By Lewis Grizzard:

I HAVEN'T UNDERSTOOD ANYTHING SINCE 1962
    AND OTHER NEKKID TRUTHS*
YOU CAN'T PUT NO BOOGIE-WOOGIE ON THE KING
    OF ROCK AND ROLL*
IF I EVER GET BACK TO GEORGIA, I'M GONNA NAIL
    MY FEET TO THE GROUND*
DON'T FORGET TO CALL YOUR MAMA ... I WISH I
    COULD CALL MINE
DOES A WILD BEAR CHIP IN THE WOODS?
CHILI DAWGS ALWAYS BARK AT NIGHT*
DON'T BEND OVER IN THE GARDEN, GRANNY, YOU
    KNOW THEM TATERS GOT EYES*
WHEN MY LOVE RETURNS FROM THE LADIES
    ROOM, WILL I BE TOO OLD TO CARE?*
MY DADDY WAS A PISTOL, AND I'M A SON OF A
    GUN
SHOOT LOW, BOYS—THEY'RE RIDIN' SHETLAND
    PONIES*
ELVIS IS DEAD AND I DON'T FEEL SO GOOD MYSELF
IF LOVE WERE OIL, I'D BE ABOUT A QUART LOW
THEY TORE OUT MY HEART AND STOMPED THAT
    SUCKER FLAT
DON'T SIT UNDER THE GRITS TREE WITH ANYONE
    ELSE BUT ME
WON'T YOU COME HOME, BILLY BOB BAILEY?
KATHY SUE LOUDERMILK, I LOVE YOU
I TOOK A LICKIN' AND KEPT ON TICKIN'*

Comedy Albums:
ON THE ROAD WITH LEWIS GRIZZARD
LEWIS GRIZZARD LIVE
LET'S HAVE A PARTY WITH LEWIS GRIZZARD
ADDICTED TO LOVE
DON'T BELIEVE I'DA TOLD THAT

*Published by Ballantine Books

I TOOK A LICKIN' AND KEPT ON TICKIN'
(And Now I Believe in Miracles)

Lewis Grizzard

BALLANTINE BOOKS • NEW YORK

Copyright © 1993 by Lewis Grizzard

All rights reserved under International and Pan-American Copyright Conventions. Published in the United States of America by Ballantine Books, a division of Random House, Inc., New York, and simultaneously in Canada by Random House of Canada Limited, Toronto.

Library of Congress Catalog Card Number: 93-30411

ISBN 0-345-39093-8

This edition is published by arrangement with Villard Books, a division of Random House, Inc. Villard Books is a registered trademark of Random House, Inc.

Manufactured in the United States of America

First Ballantine Books Edition: January 1995

10   9   8   7   6   5   4   3   2   1

To Dedra, the real survivor

ACKNOWLEDGMENTS
AND THANKS

- To everybody at Emory Hospital. God bless you.
- To my readers. I don't deserve your support.
- To friends and relatives. You were there through it all. I love you.
- To Peter Gethers. Thanks for your patience.
- To Dawn and Fran for typing and retyping.
- To James for taking care of Catfish.

✳✳✳ Introduction ✳✳✳

I'M USED TO DEADLINE PRESSURE. I ONCE COVERED
night, Central Time Zone college football games for
an Eastern Time Zone newspaper. Night, Central
Time Zone college football games usually end about
midnight, Eastern time. My deadline was ten
minutes after midnight, Eastern time.

I never missed a deadline. I forgot to put the final
score in my story a couple of times and once referred
to the Rice "Owls" as the "Horned Frogs" (that's
Texas Christian), but I never missed a deadline.

I covered the 1980 National Republican Convention in Detroit. Except for the incident at a
women's lib march where one of the female march-
ers used a cigar to burn my colleague's sport coat to
a crisp, that convention was a rather dull affair. My
nightly deadline was 10:00 P.M.

At 9:30 one night, I absolutely couldn't think of anything about which to write a column. Finally, I wrote that Gerald Ford, not George Bush, would wind us as Ronald Reagan's running mate. So I was wrong. I still made deadline.

But this book.

This book.

This is my umpteenth book—I can't remember—and I've had deadline pressure completing many of the others, too. For a book that is due out in October, which is when mine usually come out, editors want the completed manuscript approximately four years earlier.

When authors are asked if they can deliver the completed manuscript by that time, they all say sure, no problem. That's because they want their hands on the advance royalty check as quickly as possible. After they get the check, they pretty much ignore their editors—refusing to take their pleading phone calls, forgetting totally about any nonsense due dates—and simply work on their own perfectly adequate pace. My problem getting a manuscript in on time has always been that playing golf is more fun than writing a book. A *lot* more fun.

Golf isn't getting in my way this time, however. I can't play golf because, as I type this, I'm two months out of Heart Surgery from Hell, and my sternum has been wired back together after being split open for that surgery. One's sternum takes three postsurgical months for it to be able to withstand something as forceful as my golf swing, which has been known to suck small caddies, standing 150 yards down the fairway behind me, in its awesome wake.

It's the tip of the pointer finger on my right hand that is the problem with this book. And the cause of the immense deadline pressure I'm feeling. This will take some explaining:

I checked into Emory Hospital in Atlanta on March 21, 1993, for my third heart surgery in eleven years. I was born with a leaky aortic valve. In 1982, when I was thirty-five, I had my first surgery, and a porcine (hog) valve was implanted, replacing the faulty one that arrived with me on October 20, 1946, in an army hospital in Fort Benning.

That valve became infected in 1985, and it was replaced by another pig valve, which was worn out and ineffectual by March of '93, and so there I was for my third surgery.

My doctors decided it was time for a mechanical valve this time. Tissue valves such as the porcine one tend to last an average of only seven to ten years. Mechanical valves last much longer—but they tend to cause blood clotting, and strokes. A minor inconvenience, though blood-thinning drugs can cut down on the possibility of the aforementioned strokes, so the doctors tell me.

So there I am for my third surgery and my St. Jude's mechanical valve. The operation was to be as routine as a third heart-valve replacement surgery can be. The Bay of Pigs was to be a routine invasion, too.

The heart is stopped for surgery by a cooling process. During surgery, the patient's blood is pumped through the body by the heart-lung, or bypass, machine.

Monday morning, March 22, they wheeled me into surgery. I was not aware of any of this at the time, thank God. I hate having my heart stopped by a cooling process. Everything went fine, they would tell me later, until they took me off the bypass machine.

My new valve had been implanted, but my heart wouldn't start beating again. The sucker just sat there and didn't even flinch. For the next three days, great learned men and women of medicine, ones with eye charts after their names, would do everything in their power to get my heart to start beating again and get me off the machine. There was a little bit of a rush about all this because the bypass machine can only sustain life for about seventy-two hours. At that point, other organs, such as the liver and kidney, give it up, too.

For those seventy-two hours, I was desperately close to death.

"They kept telling us," said a friend who was at the hospital, "it doesn't look good. Their eyes said, 'It's over.'"

My cardiologist put it this way:

"You were as good as gone."

I'll get into what doctors described as a miracle (I lived) later, but here's what has caused there to be great deadline pressure involving this book:

Don't ask me how it happened, but during the

crisis, my heart threw off various blood clots, all but one relatively harmless. That one little devil, however, went to the tip of my right index finger, and the result was not pretty.

The tip of the finger, from the first joint upward, is completely black. I mean middle-of-the-night, Black Beauty black. My finger looks like I caught it in the door of the Chicago-to-Omaha Greyhound express.

In other words, it didn't survive the ordeal the way the entire rest of my body did. It is in basically the same condition it would be in were it suffering from frostbite, which is something one can easily get standing outside waiting for the Chicago-to-Omaha Greyhound express without one's mittens.

As soon as I noticed the revolting-looking black area, I asked the nearest doctor, "What on earth have you done to my finger?"

He explained.

Next I asked, "What is going to *happen* to my finger?"

The doctor said, "You're going to lose the tip."

Wait a minute, I thought. I came in here to have a new aortic valve placed in my heart, and suddenly I'm going to lose the tip of my finger?

"It's an outpatient procedure," he explained, nonchalantly. Why not: It wasn't *his* finger. "They deaden the finger and then take it off. You don't even have to spend the night in the hospital."

What a relief that was. I could get the tip of my finger cut off and still be home in time to watch *Wheel of Fortune* on my own television.

I've been through three heart operations now,

having my sternum split open and chest spread
from one end of the operating room to the other so
surgeons can get up to their elbows in my cardio-
vascular system, and now they're telling me, on top
of all that, I'm going to lose the tip of one of my
most precious digits?

I made a major decision about the tip of my finger shortly after the doctors explained how I was
going to have to have it chopped off. That decision
was: *My ass*.

Doctors tried to reason with me. They said the
finger could not be saved and that, as long as I was
already in the hospital, it would be much more con-
venient to go ahead and have it removed at the
time. They warned of such matters as infections.
But I held firm.

So I left the hospital a month after my surgery
with my finger unattractive but intact. They haven't
stopped trying to whack it off, however.

When I went back for my two-month checkup,
my heart was deemed strong and fit. The new valve
was working marvelously, and my cardiologist said
I was probably no more than four or five weeks
away from golf.

But the finger.

They brought a plastic surgeon by to look at it.

"What's going to happen," he said, "is the outer
black cover is going to fall off soon. What you will
be left with is a precious little amount of tissue covering the bone, and it will be very painful. But I
can put two needles in the bottom of the finger and

completely deaden it. You won't feel a thing when I take off the tip."

I didn't ask the doctor exactly how they took off tips of people's fingers, but I did assume the bulge in the pocket of his white doctor's jacket was a hatchet, which reminded me of the lines from the song about Lizzie Borden, the famous ax murderer:

"Shut the door/lock and latch it/ here comes Lizzie with a brand-new hatchet."

I stood my ground.

"Stay away from my finger," I said to the plastic surgeon.

I'm not so stupid as to think doctors are lying to me about the finger, however. It's just that they said it was a miracle I managed to live through the heart surgery and all its complications, so I'm hoping for another miracle regarding my finger.

I'm hoping that one morning I'll awaken, and it won't be black anymore. Pretty pink tissue will have replaced the hard crust that is there now. Sea Hero won the Kentucky Derby, didn't he?

But let us say that doesn't happen. Let's take the worst-case scenario. The outer crust will come off, nearly exposing the bone and causing great pain. The doctor told me that the pain would be too great for me to even *think* about typing. If that happens, I'll *have* to have the tip amputated. But, even with a prosthesis, which will give me a lot of mobility, it would be a month before I could type again.

So, I must finish this book before the tip of my finger either falls off or I lose it to Dr. Borden. The book is supposed to be released this fall, and if I'm not finished by midsummer, my unsympathetic editor tells me, there won't be enough time to get it out on schedule. (He's probably lying. I probably could write until September, and there still would be plenty of time, but I don't know if my finger will hold out that long, and worse, I don't get the other half of my advance payment until the manuscript is finished. I tried whining and begging, but even with a good excuse like a coma and a black finger editors don't go tossing away money.) So here I am in the middle of May, racing toward what I figure is to be a mid-July deadline. If something happens to my finger between now and then, I'll be dead, and so will the book.

People have asked me, "If you can't type the book, why don't you just dictate it into a dictating machine?"

It's amazing what civilians don't know about writing. My typewriter is my direct link with the gods of creativity. I *think* on the typewriter. I suppose I could write it longhand, even with the tip of my finger missing, except I haven't written anything in longhand since I was in high school. I actually have lost the ability to write intelligibly. I can print a little, but my signature looks like it belongs on the side of a cave.

No finger. No typing. No book. Lots of pressure. And there's more:

This is a very important book for me. People often ask, "Which of your books is your favorite?"

Which of your children do you like the best?

But this book is important, more so than my others, because it deals with nearly dying, which I most certainly did for those seventy-two hours at Emory.

I feel the experience has left me with a lot to share about the subject of coming close to buying that proverbial piece of pastoral real estate (in other words, croaking) and living to talk about it.

There is much to say about survival. There is much to say about the love of family and friends. There is much to say about spirituality and faith, prayer and higher beings.

Then there's smoking and drinking and eating greasy food, not to mention staying away from any doctor who could have been a brain or heart surgeon but chose instead to specialize in sticking things up people's butts. I have an awful lot to say about that, as a matter of fact.

Then there's hospital food, tubes, wires, bloodsuckers, and the fact that when a man wears one of those little gowns they give you in a hospital, when he lies down, his testicles are automatically going to show to whoever happens to be in his room. I also peed on one of my doctor's shoes one day and threw up on another's Rolex watch. I promise not to go into any sort of great detail about either of those instances, by the way. Although it is interesting exactly how I managed it.

I'm convinced, and so are a lot of others, I had no business living through my ordeal. "Miracle" has, in fact, been thrown around a lot in my direction, and there are those who even say, "You were spared for a purpose."

Was it to write this book? Was it so I could try to convey what it's like to get another chance at life? Was it so I could say to whoever might read this effort, "Before you get too down, remember you're at least still above the grass"?

Was it to try to touch all those who suffer from the condition of optical rectitis, which strikes nearly everybody on occasion? Optical rectitis? Shitty outlook on life.

Maybe this could turn into one of those self-help books that changes people's lives, like my favorite, *Success Despite Smelly Feet*.

I'm happy to be alive. I want a lot of others to feel the same way. Maybe I can forge a few grins and positive thoughts, and alleviate some OR and its cousin, constipation of the personality.

All I can do is keep my finger crossed.

✱✱✱ 1 ✱✱✱

It wasn't the first time my stepbrother, Ludlow Porch, the famous syndicated radio talk-show host from Atlanta, had asked me to do something crazy. Once, Ludlow called and asked me to be on his Atlanta television special. I figured he wanted me on to talk about my latest book, my latest marriage, or my latest idiotic real estate venture. All three, especially the last two, are usually good for a few laughs.

But no. Ludlow wanted me to come on his Atlanta television special and sing.

"What do you want me to sing?" I naturally asked him.

" 'Old Dogs, Children and Watermelon Wine,' " he answered.

No problem. I had entertained as many as eleven people, after they had all had several drinks, singing that Tom T. Hall immortal in my living room. I'm not a bad singer. Really. Especially if I don't have to hit any high notes. I have a rather deep voice, and I can growl out a country song or two without embarrassing myself. Someone once described my singing as "Tennessee Ernie Ford being cranked on a cold morning."

Ludlow said he had a band that would appear on the show; I could arrive early and practice my number with them. He assured me that the audience would love me as the eleven had before in my living room.

I arrived an hour early for the live show.

"Is the band here?" I asked Ludlow. "I want to run over my number a couple of times."

"First," Ludlow answered, "try on your costume."

"Costume?"

"It's just a cowboy outfit," he explained. "You don't want to go on television singing a country-music song in a pair of khakis, a golf shirt, and a blue blazer. Think Porter Wagoner would wear something like that?"

Porter Wagoner wears rhinestones in his navel, but I didn't see why I had to dress up like a cowboy to sing on Ludlow's show. But he insisted, and Ludlow is a lot bigger than I am.

It wasn't an ordinary cowboy's outfit. It was a cowboy outfit worthy of Liberace. The hat had a leather chin string, so it wouldn't blow off, I suppose, during any sort of bizarre cowboy sexual exercise, such as "Giddyup, Wild Pony" or "Ride the Kinky Doggie."

The shirt was worse. It featured pictures of tumbling tumbleweeds wearing happy faces. When I put on the rather furry chaps, it looked like twenty-seven cats had attached themselves to my legs. And my boots were mauve. There were spurs, of course. You can't play "Giddyup, Wild Pony" without spurs.

To make matters much, much worse, the band knew only one tune, which sounded a lot like "Satin Doll." In places. We tried my number once. I was a disaster.

"Two minutes, Mr. Grizzard," the director said suddenly. "You're on first after Mr. Porch's opening monologue."

"I'm not going to do this," I announced.

"They'll love you," the director promised, handing me a guitar.

"I don't play guitar," I protested.

"Just pretend," said the director. "The band will drown you out anyway."

Unfortunately, the band didn't drown me out. They played "Satin Doll" lightly in the background while I tried to sing a country song, dressed like Gene Autry's hairdresser.

The reviews were mixed. Some said I was awful. Others said that didn't begin to describe it.

"I'll make it up to you," Ludlow said later. "I'll get Diane [his lovely wife] to cook you a pork-chop dinner."

We had Spam croquettes. I hate my stepbrother.

Several months later, in June of 1985, Ludlow called me again.

"I won't do it," I said.

"How do you know you won't do it?" Ludlow asked me. "You don't even know what I'm going to ask you to do."

"I don't care," I said. "I won't do it. The Country Music Association is still considering suing me after your television show, and Tom T. Hall has vowed to send somebody to shoot me in the knees."

"I simply wanted to see if you wanted to go to the Soviet Union with Diane and me and a few other people," Ludlow said. "I promise you won't have to sing anything or wear a cowboy outfit."

"The Soviet Union?" I asked, incredulous. "Why in the name of God would you, I, or anybody else want to go to the Soviet Union? I hear they don't even have toilet paper over there."

"We'll take copies of your latest book," said Ludlow, ever the jokester.

Ludlow explained the deal. A group of Georgians (a "few other people" turned out to be approximately two hundred) were going on a tour of the Soviet Union for two weeks in August.

Knowing Ludlow to be the staunch anti-Communist (a former marine) and nontruster of the Evil Empire that he was, I asked the next logical question:

"What are we going to do when we get over there, poison the water supply?"

"Lewis, Lewis," he said. "This is a goodwill tour, not a Chuck Norris movie. We are going to learn about the Soviet people and their way of life. We'll be going to museums, visiting Soviet citizens' homes, and trying to bridge the gap between our two peoples. And if there's time to poison the water supply, then we'll do that, too."

My mother used to say that before we die, "We are warned. God lets you know," she would explain, "so you can get ready."

She used her own father, my granddaddy Bun, as an example. Daddy Bun, as the grandchildren called him, was seventy-three when he had a heart attack while plowing his potato patch one April afternoon on his Briggs & Stratton garden tractor. He died a week later. We learned afterward that six weeks before, he had talked to the minister of his old home church and had told him he knew he would be dying soon and wanted to make certain he was in good shape with the Lord.

"Daddy was warned," Mama explained to me. I was thirteen at the time.

I had a friend who was killed in an auto accident when I was sixteen. He was two years younger. My friend's mother had told the story of how her son had come to her a few months before his death and said, "Mama, if anything ever happens to me, please don't take me down to that cemetery. Bury me near our house."

They buried my friend at the cemetery against his wishes, but there was still that warning thing again.

There was something scary about the idea of going on that trip to the Soviet Union. I really can't explain it. I had always enjoyed travel. Obviously, there was adventure involved. And I could write columns from there and reinforce my mistrust of the "Rooskies," as my father called them. But something kept saying to me, "Don't go." Détente or no détente. Glasnost or no glasnost. They still had the KGB, didn't they? What if they bugged my room and decided I was some sort of spy, and I couldn't get out of there after the two weeks were up?

You may think I'm kidding here. I'm not. I hadn't been comfortable even in Italy, because the policemen wore funny hats. In Germany, I kept waiting for somebody in a black leather coat to walk up to me and say, "May I see your papers, please?" And I'd been to Greece. You know how they tell those don't-bend-over stories about Greece.

I suppose all this portrays me as a classic xenophobe. Actually, I'm not afraid of xenos. It's foreigners who frighten me.

Nonetheless, I signed up for the trip to the Soviet Union with Ludlow and the other two hundred. What made me decide to take all the risks I had decided were involved, was the opportunity to write columns from that mysterious place. I had grown weary of defending Ronald Reagan from the bed-wetting liberals who were attacking him, and I was just as tired of writing about my dog, Catfish, the black Lab. I needed a challenge. Plus, Ludlow said if I didn't go, I was a "chickenshit do-do pot who didn't love the Lord."

More warnings started soon after I had written the check to pay for the trip. First, the check bounced. It was an accounting error by my office, but somebody was clearly trying to tell me something.

Then I went to get my visa photograph taken along with the others going on the trip, a mixture of Georgians, young and old, none of whom seemed as leery about all this as I did. When it was my turn before the camera, the travel person in charge said, "Don't smile."

That was the first time in my life I'd ever had my photograph taken and somebody had told me *not* to smile.

"Tell the photographer to say, 'Francis Gary Powers,' and I won't," I said. The travel person had no idea what I was talking about.

I did want to know, however, "Why am I not supposed to smile?"

"You don't want to draw attention to yourself," she explained. "Passport control at the Moscow airport can be suspicious of someone with a smiling visa photograph."

As in, I supposed, anybody coming to the Soviet Union with a smile on his face has got to be up to something.

"Take no English magazines, newspapers, or books with you," we were further told, closing the lid on Ludlow's toilet-paper suggestion. All my books have been in English.

Besides the ominous warnings I've already mentioned, I had friends who said such things as:

- "Do you realize how far you're going to be from the nearest barbecue joint?"

- "Can you go three weeks without hearing one word of country music?"
- "I heard about an American guy who went to the Soviet Union once. He was never heard from again." (Later, I found out the person who said that actually had only watched a made-for-TV movie where that happened, but it was still an omen.)
- "Russian women are ugly."

That last warning didn't bother me a great deal since I wasn't going to the Soviet Union to fall into love or lust. I did know there were Russian prostitutes, however, but I made up my mind not to deal with any of them before I embarked because they also could be KGB agents with bugs. Both kinds. I did have another acquaintance, however, who knew a guy who knew a guy who had been to Moscow on a business trip and had encountered a prostitute, and he passed on the story just in case such a situation should come up during my visit:

The man on the trip, another Georgian, in Moscow for an agricultural show, met what he described as an aberration, a lovely Russian woman. He was seated in a bar in his hotel, and the woman, who spoke English, sat next to him and asked if he would buy her a drink. He obliged.

They would up in his hotel room. She explained first how she was a direct descendant of Catherine the Great. Then she explained she would offer sexual services for one hundred U.S. dollars. The man from Georgia said it was really a terrific experience to meet Russian royalty, but that he didn't happen to have that much cash on him.

The princess then spotted the man's checkbook from his hometown Georgia bank lying on a desk.

"You have traveler's checks," the princess mistakenly noted.

The man from Georgia obviously had few scruples (which sort of rhymes with rubles, but Soviets want U.S. green, which, unlike the lowly ruble, has spending power).

He said, "You're absolutely right, Your Highness," and wrote her out a hundred-dollar check on a South Georgia bank, and I presume a subsequent good time was had by all.

I took my checkbook to the Soviet Union, too, but not for any such occasion as the aforementioned. I thought I might need to bribe a Kremlin official who didn't know any more about the capitalist monetary system than Catherine the Ripped-off.

But even if I had ignored all those portents of doom, the one that should have kept me at home was the tooth. That damn wisdom tooth in the back left of my mouth.

First let me explain about the mouth and teeth in regard to people with artificial heart valves. The fastest way to get an infection in the human body is orally. Put it in your mouth, and it will go directly south, and you've got big trouble.

Any infection will go to the weakest and most unprotected part of the body first, which, in my case, would be the porcine aortic valve. Because the valve can never close as tightly as a normal valve, some of the blood, pumped out of the heart through the aorta, will leak back in and will tend to eddy around the valve rather than be sent through the body to be cleansed. The valve, if it's infected, can cause a very untidy situation known as bacterial endocarditis, which can be fatal if not treated quickly.

Even before my first valve transplant, doctors had warned me about infections and had explained to me to make certain I didn't ignore any oral problems. I was also put on a strict program whereby I had to take large doses of antibiotics for trips to the dentist, even for cleanings. A cut in the mouth could, in fact, lead to major trouble.

So I knew all that ahead of time, but there was this one situation: I hated and was deathly afraid of dentists. All dentists. This began when I was a small child and my parents sent me to the dentist for the first time in Fort Benning, Georgia, where my father was stationed at the time. Army dentists aren't known for their patience with their patients. Young recruits with bad teeth sit down in their chairs while the dentists drill and yank with no regard for the pain it might cause the yank, who must then get up out of the chair and go drill. (I couldn't help writing that. Besides, I'm still on heavy medication.)

So this army dentist was groping around my mouth, and I became extremely agitated with the situation, and this man slapped me with his free hand. He couldn't hit me with both of them because I had the other one in my mouth.

My father was a captain, and, as the story was told to me later, the dentist barely escaped court-martial for striking an officer's child, but I was scarred forever. I managed to avoid the dentist for another good five or six years when my adult teeth began to appear in my mouth, along with dreaded cavities. My parents had divorced by then, and my mother and I were living with her parents in little Moreland, Georgia. My mother taught rural first grade for a whopping $120 a month, and when it became absolutely necessary for me to go to the dentist again, she took me to a man in Hogansville, ten miles south, who had a volume dealership and didn't charge the prices the dentists in the county seat of Newnan did. They, incidentally, also had been to dental school, which is probably why they charged so much.

Many of the other children in my school had been to the Hogansville dentist before me, and upon learning of my impending visit suggested I run away from home or at least poke my eye out with a sharp stick and go to the hospital, which, they assured me would be less painful an experience than going to see this dentist, whom I now imagined as a blood-splattered, demonic bogeyman with a dull jackhammer.

The day came. I had the sharp stick two inches from my eye when my mother snatched it away from me and said, "No, you don't, young man. You're not getting off that easily."

We arrived at the dentist's office Saturday morning. It was a first-come, first-serve, first-kill opera-

tion. The walls were already lined. There were
enough kids with rotten teeth in the room to film
Deliverance. I didn't see any way they would ever
get to me. I hoped my mother eventually would lose
her patience and take me back home once we had
waited several hours.

Several hours passed. My mother would have
waited a week to save a dollar.

Few of the children ahead of me went in without
a struggle. Most of them went screaming and
carrying on and pulling the chairs on which they
had been seated. It took both parents to drag one
particular hefty young girl in.

"Esther," said her mother as they reached the
middle of the room, and Esther clung, first to her
chair, and then to one with another child in it, "every
tooth in your head is going to rot out if you
don't get in there, and you won't be able to eat."

Noting Esther's healthy size, I figured that
would do it. But Esther wouldn't budge.

"I'll just gum everything like Granddaddy," she
pleaded.

The dentist's nurse finally came out, and the
three of them managed to get Esther into the office.
I had heard the screams of other children through
the walls, not to mention the grinding of the drill,
which sounded like a hundred million terribly dis-
turbed bees, but the sounds of distress Esther
made even rattled my mother. Not enough to take
me home, unfortunately, but she did say, "I'll be
right there with you," which is what parents say

when they know their children are in for something they are glad they aren't going through themselves.

I thought of running out of the room. If I could make the woods, I figured, I would be safe. I could live there forever on blackberries, abundant in the Georgia woods. I'd wear a loincloth and have long hair. I wouldn't have any teeth, but I could gum the blackberries. Maybe I could even make friends with a bear. Grizzly Grizzard. Perfect.

But my uncles and male cousins, all hunters, would probably find me, so I threw that idea out. Only one kid was ahead of me, a thin wisp of a boy, decidedly cross-eyed, who would have no chance not being taken, forcibly or otherwise, into the chamber of pain.

They took the cross-eyed boy in. When he came out, he was still quiet, but I noticed he wasn't cross-eyed anymore. *My God,* I thought to myself, *they've drilled his eyes straight.*

It was my turn. My mother and I had sat in that waiting room for six hours to save three bucks. I sucked in a deep breath, sighed, and wished I could crap in my pants. That would have shown them all.

"Wait," I said as we walked toward the dentist's office. "I demand to see Father Murphy."

Nobody had any idea what I was talking about. They hadn't watched nearly as many movies about the Big House as I had. There weren't any Catholics this side of Atlanta anyway.

I tried one more ploy.

"Any word from the governor?" I asked.

I was in the chair. The dentist, who turned out to be a rather frail man with gnarly hands (unbitten to that point, I noticed) began probing in my mouth with that godawful picklike thing, and I began to scream.

"Hold my hand," said my mother.

I grabbed hold.

The dentist shot the Novocain through my right eyeball. His drill was dull as Florence Henderson. He drilled and he filled and I cried and screamed and bled and cut the circulation off in my mother's arm. My mouth was too full of cotton and hardware to bite anybody.

I spit blood-laden saliva out into the whirling pool of water in the ceramic receptacle next to the chair. Each time I saw the sight of the goo, I recoiled in fear, slamming the back of my head against the protruding headrest, then the drilling would soon recommence. Besides that sound, there is a smell when a drill bores into the enamel of a tooth. It is the aroma of distant, acrid smoke, like a pair of polyester slacks on fire at a bingo game in a church basement two blocks down the street.

And there is a watery mist that emanates from the drill as well, that reaches into the nose, tickling the nostril hair. But who can scratch with one hand attached to his mother and the other gripping the armrest of the chair so tightly the veins are protruding all the way to the biceps?

This was easily the worst experience of my life to date. I had not masturbated all that much to be punished in such a horrible way. Perhaps I had masturbated enough to have *one* tooth filled, but when would this madman stop? Would he not be content until he had his heinous way with every tooth in my head?

It eventually would end, of course, and my mother actually thanked the dentist for his efforts and his patience and paid in cash.

"Fiend!" I wanted to scream out at the dentist, but I was afraid he might try to give me another shot of Novocain in my other eyeball. So I went quietly, but I vowed that no matter what, I would never go to another dentist, no matter the cost in rotten and lost teeth. The train still stopped in Moreland in those days, and if I couldn't afford a ticket as a passenger, I could still hop a freight and make a new life for myself if anybody ever tried to get me to a dentist again. Or there were the four Greyhounds a day, two north to Atlanta, the other pair south to Montgomery. There also were plenty of turnip and watermelon trucks leaving Moreland daily, and in the immortal words of Marco Polo, "I don't care if I have to walk, I'm out of here."

I did manage to avoid the Hogansville dentist from there on in. The next time my mother threatened to take me to him, I ran away with a gypsy family for a year. Well, not really. I crawled under our house, got into the fetal position, and swore I would hold my breath until I was dead and not go to college if I was forced back into Dr. Thrilldrill's chair.

In order to avoid complete humiliation in high school and get a date, I did have to visit a dentist in Newnan on occasion before I left home, so all my

teeth wouldn't rot out. I was even old enough by
then not to want my mother to accompany me anymore. I held the nurse's hand. Through extensive
therapy, she managed to regain use of it in an ex-
traordinarily short period of time.

Every tooth in my head had a filling in it when
I left home for college, so I figured I was through
with dentists for the rest of my life, and my mother
would no longer be around to make me go anyway.
What a relief I felt.

We jump now all the way until 1982, when I
remarried for the third time. I married a charming
young woman, filled with social graces, who introduced me to a new sort of life, including shopping
for Gucci leather goods on Worth Avenue in Palm
Beach and wearing clothes that actually matched.

She got me into the nicer hotels when we visited
New York, she taught me the correct pronuncia-
tions of the words "beige" (I said, "bage"), "chaise"
(I said, "chase"), and "salmon" (I said "sal-mun," because there's a damn *l* in it), and there were certain
hygienic lessons as well.

Before she would marry me, for instance, she
made me cut my toenails. I always purposely kept
my toenails a little long in case I ever got caught
barefoot and needed to climb a tree or a telephone
pole.

"That won't come up in your life anymore," she
explained.

She made me put Pine-Sol in my hair to remove
my dandruff, she made me trade in what she referred to as my "Charles Nelson Reilly" Pearl Opti-

cal eyeglasses for a more stylish pair, and then one day she noticed my teeth.

Somehow, the filling between the first two, applied fifteen years earlier, had fallen out. What had resulted was a cavity between my first two teeth. It didn't bother me. Made it easier to suck in pasta, which she also taught me to say instead of calling everything spaghetti.

"You must get those teeth fixed," my wife said to me.

I continued to put it off.

Then we went to Europe. It was my first time. She had been many times.

We were in Paris, staying at the Hotel Crillon. Around the corner is the world-famous restaurant Maxim's. We went there one evening for dinner. I would show my lovely wife. I ordered caviar, hang the cost. We would scrimp when we got to Monte Carlo.

They brought eleven black fish eggs. I allowed my wife to have the extra one. When we arrived back at our hotel room in the Crillon, I smiled and said, "Well, caviar. Not bad for an old country boy like me, huh, toots?"

She recoiled in horror. I had sixty-five dollars' worth of beluga (three black fish eggs) still hung in the cavity between my front two teeth. It was all I could do to get my wife to allow me to wait until I could get home to an American dentist.

Upon returning, I did have the cavity filled, and after all these years, the dentist said many of the others needed refilling, so I was back in the chair for months. I took my antibiotics, by the way, dutifully before and after each visit.

But even as a fully grown adult, I still wasn't able to be comfortable in the dentist's chair. I had to take nitrous oxide just to sit and read a two-year-old *Newsweek* in the waiting room.

I did get all my teeth repaired, finally. It didn't make my third marriage last, but once again I thought I would be through with the dentist for a time, saving the occasional trip for a cleaning, for which I also required nitrous oxide and Novocain.

I hadn't counted on wisdom teeth, however. I knew about wisdom teeth, of course, but mine were late coming in. I didn't have my first one until I was perhaps thirty-six. But, all of a sudden, I had a back-of-the-mouthful of the suckers, and there was that one, at the far left end of my bottom row of teeth.

I had noticed it had shown some signs of decay, and my dentist had urged that I allow him to at least pull that one. But I continued to squirm and whine and put it off. I'd had teeth filled and cleaned in the past several months, but having one pulled seemed as if it would be an even more excruciating experience. I could just hear it being torn from my mouth as blood spurted from my stubborn gums.

Two weeks before I was to depart for the Soviet Union, I did have the good sense to call my doctor for a quick checkup. I don't know if the movie *Reds* had been filmed by then, so I'm also not certain I had seen the part where Warren Beatty dies in that nasty Russian hospital bed, but even if I hadn't, I knew I didn't want to become ill in a Communist country. I have some rules about things like that:

RULE NO. 1: Never become ill in any foreign country, especially a Communist one.

RULE NO. 2: Never fly an airline run by a country where a lot of its people worship cows.

RULE NO. 3: Never eat in a restaurant in a foreign country where the maître d' has a gun around his shoulder and looks like somebody who played a terrorist in a Chuck Norris movie.

Except for my heart condition, I considered myself in excellent health, but I wanted to make sure I didn't have something like pancreatitis that would flare up in Moscow. I had visions of myself with Dr. Zhivago up to his elbows in my viscera as rats scurried around the operating table, with Trotsky and Lenin assisting.

My doctor examined me thoroughly and found no evidence of pancreatitis or other diseases. He said the valve sounded like it was performing admirably as well.

There was only this one, little minor hitch to my health status. My doctor looked in my mouth, and his eyes locked upon the wisdom tooth in the back lower left of my mouth.

"Hmmmm," he said.

My doctor attended the Harvard Medical School. There's a diploma on his wall to prove it. At all fine medical schools, they teach young doctors to say, "Hmmmm." The untrained medical tongue would say, "Sheeyet" instead.

"That wisdom tooth is beginning to look a little bad," said my doctor. "You really ought to have it extracted before your trip. It could become a seed-bed for an infection."

The intelligent individual, one who also had never been slapped by an army dentist or who had never been to Hogansville, Georgia, for dental treatment, would have immediately gone to his or her dentist, had the wisdom tooth removed (I prefer that word to "extracted," as I do any other term whatsoever to "root canal"), even if there was no painkiller within thirty miles. "Infection" was the key word here. You think Warren Beatty was sick. What about me with bacterial endocarditis in the Soviet Union?

"Hmmmmski," said the Soviet doctor as he looked down upon the dying capitalist, writhing in pain as the rats. . . .

But I didn't go to the dentist. I didn't have the tooth taken out. The only thing I can say in my defense was I wasn't yet forty at the time and was still immortal.

Most individuals do not consider themselves capable of dying until they are forty. I certainly didn't. I had lived through one heart surgery and three marriages by that point in my life, anyway, so what was I supposed to think?

Plus, my dentist probably wouldn't have been able to work me in anyway, and I had all that packing to do, and I had to take my dog to the vet, and I was concerned about the threat of global warming and what they're doing to the rain forest, and I was afraid.

Yes, afraid. Dentists still frighten me more than heart surgeons. I'd managed to be able to have my teeth cleaned and filled with some degree of manliness by this time, but when I thought about having a dentist reach into my mouth with some sort of plierlike tool and actually wrench a tooth from its position when such a tooth probably would resist being wrenched from its position, when I thought again of spurting blood and roots and nerves and splitting gums, I cowered in horror.

And one more thing: There was a religious angle. I still have my tonsils and my appendix. And my gallbladder. I figure God wouldn't have put in those things if he hadn't had a purpose for them. Same with wisdom teeth.

"God doesn't want me to have my wisdom tooth removed," I said to myself, and sent in a love offering to the Little Lost Sheep Fund of the Reverend Ernest Ainsley as an insurance policy.

I went to the Soviet Union for a two-week trip with a bad wisdom tooth is what I did. All that concern about getting sick in a Communist country, and I still boarded an airplane and flew to the Soviet Union with a wisdom tooth that could cause an infection that could go straight to my heart and infect my porcine aortic valve.

It was the worst mistake of my life. It came close

to killing me then. It would come even closer to killing me eight years later.

The title of this book should really be *The Dumb S.O.B. Deserved to Die*.

✳✳✳ 2 ✳✳✳

THEY TOLD ME THE COLOR SCHEME: BLUE WAS MOS-
cow Police. Brown was army. Green was KGB. At
the Moscow airport, the person behind the glass
booth at the passport-control window was in a
green uniform.

He was a pencil-neck geek with zits all over his
face, just a kid. His collar was too big for his thin
neck, and he was about as frightening as Opie Tay-
lor.

I didn't expect this. I wasn't ready for this. I had
my nonsmiling visa photograph. I had practiced my
stern look in the rest room of the flight from Frankfurt to Moscow. I wasn't going to back down, by
God. When the steel-eyed KGB agent behind the
glass booth at passport control asked me, "May I

see your papers, please?" and reached for the black gloves, I was going to stare back at him.

"Hell, yes, I'm eyeballing you, Ivan," I was going to say. "I'm from America, where you can look another man in the eye, where we're not afraid to speak up and stand up for what we believe in."

Instead, I entered the Evil Empire for the first time with this skinny kid in dire need of a good dose of Clearasil checking my papers.

I was disappointed. I really was. Opie waved me on without thought, and Barney and Goober met me at customs. These two characters went through my three bags and manual typewriter case, and all they could find to question me about was one box of Band-Aids and the then-new, 1985, just-off-the-press University of Georgia football media guide with head coach Vince Dooley's picture on the cover.

First the Band-Aids. These guys hadn't seen a box of Band-Aids before? They didn't speak English, of course. They continued to wave the box of Band-Aids in my face and rattle on, but at least not threateningly. They seemed more confused than anything else.

Finally, I gestured to allow me to hold the box of Band-Aids. I took one out of the box. I pulled the string on the wrapper, took out the Band-Aid, and applied it to the back of my hand.

The two customs agents laughed. They then each pulled out a Band-Aid, each of them pulled their red strings, and miraculously, off came the wrappers. They put their Band-Aids on the backs of their hands, compared them, and then had an even bigger laugh. I think they thought they were some sort of decadent Western marital aid.

The Georgia football brochure was much more complicated. First, some background.

Dooley had been very successful winning football games at Georgia and had decided he might even try a run at becoming governor or United States senator. Speculating on Dooley's plans had kept the state's press busy for years.

The coach, during all this speculation, learned an important lesson. Dealing with the sporting press is one thing; they only want you fired if a nineteen-year-old drops a pass. The political press wants you dead.

That group of sharks began to circle the coach. Nothing of any substance was ever reported, but Dooley obviously realized he didn't have the belly for this sort of scrutiny he and his family would face during a political campaign, so he had announced he would not seek public office and would stick to coaching.

The new brochure had arrived at my house the day I flew to Moscow. I put it in one of the bags I carried onto the plane to read during the flight. Never did I think it would cause a problem with Soviet customs. The brochure was the only publication of any sort I had in my possession. The second the two customs agents saw it, they began to say, "Politico, politico!"

For the first time, I knew what they were talking about. We had been warned, I mentioned earlier, not to bring any sort of English-language newspaper or magazines. I thought it would have been a delight to smuggle in a *National Enquirer* so the Soviets would learn of the kangaroo that gave birth to human twins or that Hitler had been found alive on the moon, but that was simply a fantasy.

I argued with the two customs agents. Smart. I realized later, all they probably would have had to have done was snap their fingers and had me taken away. I wasn't stupid enough to believe all green-clad officials around me were Opie Taylors.

Still, I argued.

I said, "No politico. No politico. Fuutball. Fuutball."

This continued for a couple of salvos. Then I had a great line. Unfortunately, I arrived a day after the rest of the visiting Georgians because of a previous scheduling conflict, so there was nobody around who could appreciate it.

They said, "Politico, politico!" again, and I said: "It was in all the papers. Dooley decided not to run."

They kept my University of Georgia football brochure as well as those two Band-Aids, but they did let me go.

I took a cab to my hotel—the Comrade Hilton—in Moscow and located the rest of the group, including my stepbrother, Ludlow, who had already spent one night in the hotel. He said to me, "How did you talk me into coming here?"

This isn't a book about my trip to the Soviet Union, but, for the record, even if I'd been in the very pink of health, this still would have ranked as one of the all-time nightmares of my life. I'm going to be as brief as I possibly can about what I found to be the mother of all travel hemorrhoids:

Soviet Hotels

First, I'll say something nice about them. Not once did anybody attempt to knife me while I was in the shower.

The shower: If any water did happen to come out, it came out a trickle at a time, a *cold* trickle. "You couldn't wash a gnat's ass in mine," said one of our more clever traveling companions.

There was no soap. I seemed to recall somebody mentioning I should bring soap. There was one towel. We were in the Comrade Hilton in Moscow for a week. That was my towel. But why would I need another one? I never got wet anyway.

There was no shower curtain. Why would I need a shower curtain? There was no water to get onto the floor.

The toilet: Ludlow finally figured out how to flush his and told me. You pulled the shades down on the one window in your room. Don't ask me why that's the way you flush a toilet in a Russian hotel bathroom. And don't ask me how a country that can't figure out a lot easier way to flush a toilet can put a man in space, either. Maybe they *didn't* put a man in space. My grandmother said *we* didn't ei-

ther, that it was some kind of trick. She believed
pro wrestling was real, too, by the way.

There was, however, some toilet paper next to
the toilet in my Moscow hotel room. This wasn't exactly Charmin we were dealing with. The maid not
only scrubbed the floors with it one morning, but I
also later noticed a taxi driver on the street using
what looked exactly like another piece as a patch
for a puncture on one of his tires.

My bed was a cot. It had a pillow and a sheet and
a blanket, but it was still a cot. There was a desk
in the room with a lamp and a telephone on it. The
lamp was where the KGB bug was, I was certain,
but it could have been in the shower head, which is
why no water came out. There was a wooden chair
that went with the wooden desk. I didn't dare use
the telephone, so I don't know if it worked or not. I
knew the line was tapped, of course, plus, in the
movie *Telefon*, with Charles Bronson as a KGB
agent, one blew up.

There was no carpet, of course. There was no rug,
either, and I don't remember anything about the
wallpaper. I was too busy trying to figure out how
to cut off the ceiling fan that was last oiled before
Stalin started executing whoever it was who invented Soviet toilet paper, and deservedly so, I
might add.

Soviet Food

Meat, potatoes, cabbage, for lunch and dinner. But there was some variety. For one meal, the meat would be on the left, the potatoes in the center, the cabbage on the right. For the next meal, the cabbage would be on the left, the meat in the middle, the potatoes on the right.

We were never quite sure about the identity of the meat. For one meal, the meat was gray. I'd never eaten gray meat. I still haven't.

Breakfast probably was the best meal. The eggs did at least have a yellowish tint, and they did serve some excellent sweet rolls. Coffee was the problem. You couldn't have any until breakfast was over. I begged for coffee before breakfast, but I never got it.

What we did have with our breakfast was bottled water. Some in our group took it back to their rooms and bathed in it.

Soviet Bars

Stoli. Neat. Otherwise, bad champagne and worse beer.

Soviet Travel

I flew Aeroflot. From Moscow to Vilnius, Lithuania. Put some wings on a Greyhound bus, and the
sucker can, in fact, fly.

We also took a couple of overnight train rides,
from Vilnius to Leningrad and then from Leningrad back to Moscow. I felt like I was being transferred to the front. It was August, so we didn't
freeze. We sweltered instead. Once I had a flat tire
on a rural Georgia road, and I had no spare. A guy
picked me up with a truck he later explained was
loaded with chicken guts he was taking to a cat-
food factory or a ship, bound for a Russian hotel. I
forget which. It was a better, and less smelly, ride
than on the Soviet train.

Soviet Shopping

Here's how bad things were. I went into Moscow's largest store, GUM. What I remember most
was a head-high stack of shoes. Just shoes. Black
shoes and brown shoes, loafers and lace-ups, men's
and women's shoes. The shoes were not in pairs,
however. The idea, I supposed, was to grope down
through there in hope of finding two shoes that resembled one another. If they were both the same
size, you've had a very successful shopping day.

Most food-store bins were empty, but you've
heard all those stories. Want to buy souvenirs to
take home? You had three choices: a bottle of lime

Stoli, a fur hat, or dolls in a stack, the kind that keep getting smaller as you take off the top one.

The Soviet People

We all felt sorry for the average Soviet citizen. Very few spoke English, of course, but most tried to help. Even the guards around the Kremlin were fairly accessible, except for the one who pointed a machine gun at me and told me I couldn't sit down on a curb near Lenin's tomb. I *guess* that's what he was saying to me. Regardless, I got up off the curb and was on my way to seek refuge in the U.S. embassy until Ludlow told me he didn't think they shot people for sitting on the wrong curb, not even in the Soviet Union.

"There you go again," he said, "listening to too many Reagan Saturday broadcasts on public radio."

The most remarkable experience we had was in Vilnius. Vilnius means "City of Churches." Here is how the Soviets handled that.

They turned many of the Vilnius churches, some centuries old, into museums of atheism. That's exactly how they were billed in sight-seeing brochures: "Museums of Atheism."

The exhibits inside were devoted to showing the farce of the world's religions. One felt as if the world had been turned inside out in one of those places. When the Lithuanians claimed their inde-

pendence, years later, international news has
rarely had such a profound, uplifting effect on me.

At breakfast at our Vilnius hotel one Sunday
(slightly better lodging than in Moscow), somebody
passed the word along that he had learned there
actually was a Baptist church in Vilnius. Somebody
asked and got directions. Maybe thirty of us piled
into cabs and went to the church.

It was a small concrete building in a neighbor-
hood of small houses. Members of the church
milled about outside, waiting for the service to begin. We found a man who spoke English. He explained that before the 1980 Olympics in Moscow,
the government actually built the church for the
Baptists.

"They wanted to make it look good here," he explained.

I supposed that after the Olympics, the little
church had sort of gotten lost in the bureaucracy
and continued to exist because nobody really noticed it.

We heard an organ. The Lithuanians began to
file into the church. We waited outside, a bit un-
sure of ourselves. But the man said, as we lingered,
"Please come inside and worship God with us."

There was a pulpit and a choir area. But there
were no pews, just wooden chairs, most of which
were occupied by older women in homemade print
dresses with scarves over their heads. A number
were World War II widows, I thought. The few men
in the church were sitting in the choir area.

We all went to the back of the church, against

the rear wall. Before the service began, the old women got out of their chairs and motioned for us to come forward and take them. We were all reluctant to do so, of course.

Again, the English-speaking man came to us and said, "Do as they say, please; it is their way of welcoming you to our church."

We took the seats.

The choir, singing along with the organ, was startlingly good. There were no hymnals, but I didn't need one to recognize the melody of "Sweet Hour of Prayer," followed by "The Old Rugged Cross." Every American cried unabashedly. I will never forget a young tenor in the choir singing out so sweetly, as an infant crawled about in his arms.

☞ ♥ ☜

I mentioned train rides in the Soviet Union. The one that's relevant to the miracle that occurred eight years later was ten days into our trip, between Vilnius, Lithuania, and Leningrad, an allnighter.

At our pre-train dinner, I ate my potatoes on the right and my cabbage in the middle, but I left the gray meat. The only gray animal I could think of right off was an elephant, which did remind me of the elephant diet my stepbrother Ludlow claimed to have been on once.

"I can have one elephant a week, cooked any way I want," Ludlow explained, "but I have to catch my own elephant." Ludlow remains a rather large individual.

The train was to leave at seven and arrive in Leningrad the next morning at eight. We received our compartment assignments at dinner. I was in one with Ludlow and his wife, Diane.

The trip got off to a bad start for me. Looking back, it could have been a lot worse. Ludlow, Diane, and I were in a car near the front of the very long train. In our group was a delightful, energetic eightyish widow from Macon, Georgia. As the train stood in the station, with the door to our compartment open due to the heat, I noticed the lady from Macon standing outside with all her bags.

"I can't find my compartment," she said.

Some checking unearthed the fact that her compartment was in a car way toward the rear of the train.

"I'll take you back there," said the last Boy Scout, me.

I picked up the bags and suggested it would be easier for us to walk outside the train on the platform than through the cars. It would never have occurred to me that the train would have left in a million years without Lewis McDonald Grizzard, Jr., on it.

The train started to move without me and the elderly lady from Macon on it.

All my bags were in my compartment. My passport was in there. All my funds, too. The train was picking up speed.

Each car of the train had an attendant whose job it was to make tea and snarl. I noticed a large Soviet female attendant standing in the door of one of the cars.

"Quick!" I said to the lady, "jump into that car."

The second she started toward the door, the unfriendly fat Soviet attendant began screaming, *"Nyet! Nyet!"* and tried to block her way.

What would I do with no money and no passport and an eighty-year-old American lady in Vilnius, Lithuania, if the train left us?

I threw the bags at the attendant. She caught one square in her ample midsection, and it pushed her back from the door. Then we jumped on the train. The eighty-year-old lady was surprisingly quick, I might add. The attendant recovered and was furious at me. We stood face-to-face, and she started speaking to me in a loud, irate voice. I figured she was cursing me in Russian. So I asked the lady from Macon to please cover her ears and began cursing the attendant in English.

Eventually, we came to an agreement—we both saw the idiocy of cursing one another in a language the other couldn't understand—and I located the lady's compartment. It turned out to be five cars back from my own. I began the trip back to the head of the train to my compartment. Soviet passengers filled the narrow passageways, seeking relief from the heat of their own compartments.

I *know* these people would have used deodorant if it were available to them. I really believe that in my heart.

Ludlow and Diane and I decided the smart thing to do would be to see if we could go to sleep. Not only were we hot, but we were very hungry by now, too.

"I could eat an elephant," said Ludlow.

I took the top bunk on the other side of the compartment from Ludlow and Diane. We had opened the window as night came. The breeze began to cool the compartment. The rail bed seemed to smooth out a bit in the countryside, and I managed to fall asleep.

In the early hours of the next morning, I awakened. I was sick. As a dog. As a goat. As an elephant who has just realized he's dinner.

I was sick to my stomach. I was sick to my head. I was congested. I had a fever. My back hurt. My legs hurt. Everything hurt. My first thought was that the fat attendant had slipped in during the night and poisoned me. But I was too sick for poison. Poison that could make you this sick would have killed me by then.

I awakened Diane, who had medicine.

I took two aspirin, ate four Tums, drank a half-bottle of Pepto-Bismol, and took four of her Midols. But none of that offered any relief. By the time we got off the train and checked into our Leningrad hotel, I was a dry-heaving, head-hurting, stomach-cramping shell of a human being.

We had a doctor in our group. She gave me more aspirin and asked if I had diarrhea, which, surprisingly, I did not. I think it was the only bad thing in the world that I didn't have. She suggested I remain in my hotel room and rest, which I did.

I decided that afternoon that I had a bad cold.

That's what it had to be. I had slept with that night air hitting me in the train. Everybody knows night air causes colds.

By the evening, I actually felt a lot better and went out sight-seeing. I would muddle through somehow, especially since the doctor, I learned, would be with us on the trip.

There is a little voice inside all of us that speaks when we are in various stages of crisis. There is one that speaks to us from our bowels. Let us call it Mr. Bowel Voice.

Mr. Bowel Voice first spoke to me after we'd been on the boat bound for the summer palace for about fifteen minutes. He said, "Lewis, you may have made a rather large mistake by coming on this trip."

He spoke to me again a few minutes later, and said, "What is ice made out of, Mr. College Graduate?"

By the time we actually reached the palace, he said, "Son, you'd better find yourself a rest room as quickly as is humanly possible."

I never really got to see much of Peter the Great's summer palace that day, but I do know that it was huge. Bigger than Dollywood, I'm certain. And there were many, many people there. I remember that.

Upon seeing the size of the place and the number of visitors there, as a matter of fact, I recall thinking, They've got to have rest rooms everywhere.

So I started looking for one.

The voice said, "Do hurry."

I broke into a trot. Or a Trotsky as they call it over there.

I couldn't find a rest room.

Mr. Bowel Voice said, "It's too late for that. Just find cover."

I noticed some woods. Perhaps I could make it to them. If not, how would I ever be able to get back on that boat with all those people who actually knew my name and where I lived?

Then I spotted a small outbuilding. I saw a man emerge. I went in. It was, in fact, a rest room. Well, sort of a rest room. I'd never seen a rest room quite like this one, but we were talking a matter of seconds by this time.

There was no commode in this rest room. What was there were two metal footholders, sitting up at an angle. Sort of like the ones at shoeshine stands. To the back of the footholders was a hole in the floor. A small amount of water ran into the hole.

It didn't take me very long to figure out what I was supposed to do, and this time I wouldn't even have to try to figure out how the thing flushed.

I took my stance on the footholders. Then, like a bolt, the thought it me: Is there any toilet paper in this place? They had told me before the trip I might want to take some toilet paper with me when I went out of my hotel because you just never knew, but I had ignored all that, thinking I could always hold it until I got back to the hotel, but how was I to know they make ice out of water in the Soviet Union?

There was no toilet paper. There was nothing.

Mr. Bowel Voice said, "I know what you're thinking, and do not try it."

This is a true story. I swear it:

I left the little building, in all my pain and agony, finding abdominal strength from some source unknown, and went searching for some semblance of toilet paper. I looked for a discarded copy of *Pravda*, a souvenir stand to purchase a Russian map, and I tried in vain to buy a tire with several punctures on it from a taxi driver.

What saved me was this: They were selling ice-cream cones wrapped in paper at the palace, and many had simply thrown their wrappers upon the ground. I went around picking up those little wrappers, and once I figured I had enough, I went back to the little building and saved myself a great deal of embarrassment.

"You are one lucky son of a bitch," said Mr. Bowel Voice.

I never ventured far from my hotel room and the government-issue tissue after that. Four days later, we took the train from Leningrad to Moscow, also overnight, and I made damn certain there were toilet facilities with some of that chicken-scratch paper, about which I was no longer complaining.

I made another key mistake in this sorrowful saga, that last day in Moscow. From the rail station, we checked into another hotel for the day. Our flight left for the return to Frankfurt at seven that evening. The itinerary called for us to spend the evening in Frankfurt, then take a late-morning flight back to Atlanta.

But not me. Before leaving home, I had arranged
to play golf at the Old Course in St. Andrews, Scotland, the very birthplace of golf. I would fly back to
Frankfurt with the rest of the group, then leave
them to go on to London and then on to St. Andrews.

An intelligent person, a quite sick individual—
would have realized the prudent thing to do would
be to get back home as quickly as possible to seek
medical assistance. But, at this point, I still believed that what I had was a cold. Okay, maybe it
was some sort of exotic Russian flu, but I still believed it was something that would pass any day. I
had never been to St. Andrews at that point, and
no amount of Mr. Bowel Voice's talking, no fevers,
no chills, no anything, was going to keep me from
the trip.

I spent the last day in Moscow between my hotel
bed and the toilet. Finally, the bus came for the airport. Two weeks in the Soviet Union was over.

"If you ever suggest I do anything like this
again," I said to Ludlow, "I'm going to write a column saying you don't love the Lord, and you eat
instant grits."

The Lufthansa jet lifted off the runway. A spon-
taneous cheer broke out among the passengers.

My room wasn't ready at the Hyde Park Hotel in
London. I was too sick to do anything else but sit
down at a table in the lobby, where a very polite
man brought me a cup of tea. I was to take an early
train the next morning to Edinburgh and then on
to St. Andrews for my round of golf. Then I would

travel back to London and on back to Atlanta on a
Delta flight out of Gatwick.

I had five cups of tea before they finally came
and escorted me to my room. The wait had not been
easy. I was tired and irritable atop everything else
that was wrong with me.

But, as the case had been in the Frankfurt hotel
the evening before, at least I was in a free country
again, the toilet paper was more what I was used
to, there was room service, the water came out of
the shower head, and there were large towels, *three*
of them. I ordered three more, then I wallowed in
the Western bath decadence I had missed for two
weeks.

I crawled into my bed and turned on the television. Joan Rivers was a guest on what the British
call a chat show.

I ordered a steak from room service, certain that
a good, nongray steak would make me feel better.
But I couldn't eat it. The salad wouldn't go down,
either. Neither the bread.

There is a point, I suppose, when any of us who
have been stricken with an illness know for sure
whether or not it is something that will pass or
whether it is much more serious than that and it is
time to, well, get off the pot.

About the time Joan Rivers was going off the
chat show, that latter realization came to me.

I didn't have a bad cold. I didn't have the flu.
This wasn't going to go away. I put my hand to
my forehead. I was afire. I was weak and dizzy. I
was even having trouble focusing my eyes. And I

was four thousand miles from home in a London
hotel room.

And then I remembered the tooth. Just then—
after a week of this—I remembered the tooth. I
went to the bathroom and looked at it in the mirror. It really didn't look any worse than it had the
last time I'd looked at it at home, but over a month
had passed since my doctor had warned it could be
the source of an infection, and I had done absolutely nothing about it. The panic hit with a terri-
ble force.

"I could be dying," I said aloud.

I don't think I've ever felt as lonely as I did at
that moment.

I called the front desk and told them I needed to
see the house doctor as soon as possible. He arrived
a half hour later. It was early evening.

And then there I was in a London hospital with
a man taking my blood. The hotel doctor had called
am ambulance.

"Your fever is our main concern," another doctor
said.

I didn't wait a moment longer. I gave him my
complete medical history and told him about my
valve and my tooth.

"Hmmmm," he muttered in a British accent, and
I swear it's possible to mutter "hmmmm" in a British accent. I just can't spell how it sounds.

I also gave him my doctor's name and phone
number in Atlanta. The doctor went to phone him,
another house passed, and the man came back for
more blood.

Another hour later, the doctor returned and said he had spoken with my physician in Atlanta, but they needed to do even more extensive blood studies before there could be further diagnosis. I had mentioned to him I had been in the Soviet Union the previous two weeks. He asked me if I had been east of the Urals.

"I don't think so," I said. I wasn't certain where the Urals were, but I hadn't remembered passing them.

"Just making sure," he said. "There are some nasty bugs out there."

A woman brought my dinner with some tea. The meat looked like ham. The bread was harder than Chinese arithmetic. I think the vegetable was broccoli. I didn't even try to eat. I asked for coffee to replace the tea.

The woman looked at me like I was crazy, and I was left in my room alone for yet another hour. I made another mistake. I began to think again.

I recalled my doctor in Atlanta telling me what usually happened to people with bacterial endocarditis was that they had to be hospitalized for up to six weeks to take intravenous antibiotics. I didn't want to be in any hospital for six weeks, much less a British hospital. It certainly was better than a Soviet hospital, of course, but I was still in a foreign country that didn't want to serve me any coffee.

Obviously, I had no further thoughts of playing golf in St. Andrews at that point, but it did occur to me it was late August and that Georgia was to begin its 1985 football season against Alabama on Labor Day night in Athens on national television and that if I had to stay in London for six weeks for treatment, I'd not only miss that, I would miss half the season. Priorities. I've got some strange ones.

It was maybe nine, London time, when the doctor returned to my room and said that, yes, I did have some sort of infection, but they didn't know what sort it was or exactly what was the source.

My first question was, "Can I go home?"

"I really don't think it would be safe for you to travel at this point," he replied.

I made up my mind at that very moment. I was out of here.

Naturally, I didn't tell the doctor that.

I simply decided that, no matter how sick I was, the next morning, I was leaving that hospital, getting to Gatwick Airport, and getting on an airplane and flying back to Atlanta.

"I'm not staying in a foreign country during football season," I said to myself, feeling quite patriotic as a matter of fact.

I spent a restful night. They apparently gave me a sleeping aid. Early the following morning, another woman brought my alleged breakfast and more tea, both of which I ignored. She left the room. I didn't know how much time I had before a nurse or a doctor would come through the door. Still weak and sick, but with a fourth-quarter will, I got out of the bed, dressed, gathered up a few belongings, and walked out of my room.

I was aware my bags had been brought to the

hospital from the hotel. The trick was finding them. There was also the matter of the bill, but I didn't want to risk alerting anyone I was making my getaway. I'd send them a check later.

The hospital was only two stories high, and I was on the first floor. As I crept down the hallway, I noticed a man mopping the floor. I figured it was safe to ask him where he thought bags might be stored.

He suggested a closet near the front entrance of the building. I located the closet. Doctors and nurses were about, but none recognized me. Brazenly, I entered the closet. Sure enough, there were my bags.

I picked them up and simply walked out the door. Once on the street, I had no idea where in London I happened to be, but I did know there was an eleven o'clock flight to Atlanta, and I hailed a cab and said, "Gatwick."

Gatwick is forever out of London, but I arrived an hour and a half before the flight. There was Medallion class space available. I went to the telephone and awakened a friend at home.

"I'm sick, and I may be dying," I said, "but my young ass is out of here. Have somebody meet me at the airport and then call my doctor and tell him I'll come straight to his office."

The hour and a half crept, and I began to worry about leaving the hospital and not paying the bill. I half expected one of those blaring sirens and representatives from Scotland Yard chasing me through the airport as I tried to make the plane. So, taking the advice of a late uncle—"When in doubt, go to the bar"—I went to the bar and ordered a vodka and orange juice. It's amazing how vodka and orange juice will go down a dying man easier than steak and hospital ham will.

I lived through the nine-hour flight. Barely. I felt so bad, I couldn't hold up my head, so I put it on a seat arm and drank more vodka and orange juice through a straw. My attitude, if not my heart, was improving with every mile we drew closer to home. So I probably had bacterial endocarditis, I thought. I can catch up on a lot of reading during the six weeks in the hospital. At least I'd be able to hear the Georgia games on the radio and watch those that were to be televised.

Back in Atlanta's Northside Hospital, it took them three days to find out that my infection was going to kill me unless drastic measures were taken, so they transferred me back to Emory. I remember the ambulance ride. The next thing I recall is my Emory cardiologist, Willis Hurst, and the surgeon, Ellis Jones, who had replaced my earlier heart valve, standing over my bed saying, "We hate to have to put in another valve, Lewis, but we don't have any other choice."

It was the tooth.

I spoke with my surgeon again a couple of days after he had implanted my second porcine valve.

He said, "The infection already had eaten a hole in the wall of your heart. I had to patch. You probably wouldn't have made it another twenty-four hours."

My cardiologist explained that the infection in

the aorta was so advanced it took all the surgeon's skills just to be able to attach the valve in place.

Then they came and wheeled me away and took out *all* my wisdom teeth.

I will be forevermore indebted to my dentist and my doctor for never saying then—and they still haven't said—"I told you so."

I remained at Emory for another month, taking massive doses of intravenous antibiotics. My blood had to be checked a couple of times each day during that period, too, and it was during that time I went through a hell on earth, much worse than the two previous surgeries, worse even than *any* dental work I'd previously had. I had to endure the Time of the Needle.

*** 3 ***

THE FIRST COUPLE OF HUNDRED TIMES I HAD BLOOD drawn from my body, I took it quite well.

But I had never had a massive infection before. As I said, after my second operation, they kept me in Emory for a month to keep an eye on the infection and feed me antibiotics.

They also drew a lot of blood. That's not exactly right. They drew *oceans* of blood. They drew blood morning, noon, afternoon, and night. The first time I noticed I was about to have a problem with all this was when a phlebotomist (blood drawer, which I later began to refer to as "bloodsucker") came into my room, pulled out her needle, and I felt like I was going to throw up.

Because I am a nice person, I said to the phlebotomist, "I just think I ought to warn you, I might be about to toss here."

The feeling did go away, however, so the bloodsucker got her tubeful and went on her way, her uniform still clean.

But as the days and the needles continued, a number of things began to happen. One was that bloodsuckers began to show up in my room two at a time.

One would stick me and get a supply. The other would wait patiently, stick again, and then get another supply. There would be two sticks instead of one, in other words, and this began to happen at least twice a day.

I had an easy solution for that.

The next time two came into my hospital room, I said, "Why don't one of you stick me and then get enough blood for the both of you? Saves me a stick, and you a lot of time."

Would could be more simple?

"Can't do that," I was told.

Naturally, I asked why.

I got something about part of the blood going to one lab and the other part going to another lab, and although it wasn't mentioned, it probably had something to do with bloodsucker union rules, too.

Something worse began to happen after that. It began to get more difficult for bloodsuckers to get blood out of my veins. I wasn't blessed with large veins. Some people are. A bloodsucker can tap a large vein, and it will jump out of the skin and beg to be stuck.

Not mine.

The more times they were stuck, the more they began to run for cover as soon as they saw somebody walk into the room with a needle.

A bloodsucker explained it to me one day:

"The more your veins are stuck," she said, "the harder it is to get blood from them."

"I was getting that idea, Drac," I said.

So the bloodsuckers kept coming to my room, and my veins kept trying to run away from their ghastly needles. And when bloodsuckers can't get a vein to give blood quickly, they probe. And that hurts.

Not only did my veins begin to run for cover, they began to refuse to give up any of their precious bodily fluids no matter how much probing was done to them. This is called "blowing out" a vein.

"This one's blown out," I can still hear the bloodsuckers saying.

Probe. Probe. I threatened to kill at least seven bloodsuckers if they didn't get those lances out of me during probing time.

I want to also point out that during all this bloodsucking, I was hooked to an I.V. drip of antibiotics, which meant another large needle was in one of my hands at all times. This had to be changed once every four or five days, and that had become a problem for I.V. personnel, too. They had to do their own probing to get an I.V. needle to stick and hold to a vein.

"Why don't you just stick this son of a bitch in my eyeball?" I asked an I.V.'er one day.

"Only kidding!" I had to scream as I grabbed her

wrist with my free hand. People who stick other people for a living, I was learning, didn't care where they stuck, as long as they did, in fact, make a puncture somewhere. These people would invite Charles Manson to speak at their annual convention if the authorities would let him out of jail.

A war broke out between me and the I.V.'ers and bloodsuckers.

I won the I.V. war. A doctor from the infectious disease department was in my room one day when a nurse came in to reneedle me. She couldn't get it to hold in any of the veins that were still available in either of my hands. The rest were so full of holes they resembled a tire on a Russian taxi.

"If I can't get this vein, I could try an eyeball," the nurse said to the doctor, who did seem to be looking on with at least a bit of compassion, rare, it seemed to me, for a doctor witnessing pain.

Then the doctor said, "Here, let me do it."

He slipped the I.V. needle into a vein in a second. I barely noticed it.

"Your name, kind sir?" I asked the doctor. He told me.

"Doctor," I said, "let me put it to you this way. I will, under no conditions, ever allow anybody but yourself to attempt to insert an I.V. needle inside me. I realize this is going to put some undue burden on you, but, knowing of your obvious kindness and devotion to the easing of human suffering, I also know you will accept this, my humble, yet insistent, plea."

It was a shame about the man missing his own

daughter's wedding a couple of weeks later, but he had promised to do all my I.V.'s if I promised to take the knife (smuggled off my breakfast tray for just such a desperate situation) from the neck of the nurse.

I lost the bloodsucker war. I tried violence with them, too. They stopped bringing knives with my meal trays after the incident with the nurse, but I did hit a bloodsucker over the head with the blunt end of a spoon after she had probed for what I considered to be much too long a time. Anything over a second was my absolute limit.

But they kept coming, these fanged, needle-packing hatefuls. I'd knee one in the groin, whomp another with a bedpan, but they reminded me of what my father had said of fighting the Chinese in the Korean War.

"You kill one, a thousand come to take his place."

This is not to say I didn't find a few bloodsuckers who would at least *try* not to hurt me. I even made a deal with a few of them. All I asked, and the few agreed, if they didn't hit something that would gush immediately, not to hang around in there in my hand, wrist, or arm doing all that probing.

"Just get on out, and we'll stick somewhere else," I pleaded. These individuals I did not attempt to maim in any manner.

I couldn't get others to do that, however, especially those who would come to take blood out of me for the first time.

I had tried to work the same deal I had worked with the I.V. doctor with a few of the bloodsuckers. I wanted them, and only them, to take my blood. But the new I.V. went in once every several days, not once every several hours, so I failed in that effort.

At least once a day, I would get a bloodsucker who'd never tried to get blood out of me. We are talking worst-possible scenario here.

Bloodsuckers, I found out, are a proud lot. They coined the phrase about getting blood out of a turnip. I would say to a bloodsucker I had never seen before:

"Well, hello there. Now, before we begin, allow me to explain that the odds are about ninety-nine to one that you're going to find it nearly impossible to get blood out of me. Many have come before you, and many have wished they had gone into hotel management instead of blood-sucking."

This simply made them more determined and more likely to probe in a vein until sundown in an effort to get it to give forth. By the time I left the hospital, I figured I'd had the blood of three fully grown men extracted from me, at the cost of great pain and anxiety. I also had several personal-injury lawsuits against me. I found another airline I wouldn't fly, as well—SwissAir. Their symbol is a red cross.

☞ ♥ ☜

By the first of the year in 1986, I had fully recovered from operation No. 2. In three years, I'd gone through two heart surgeries and was still standing. I'd made it through one that was elective and through one that was a grave emergency. I fully realized I had another porcine valve, and that if I lived long enough, it eventually would have to be replaced, too, but I'd heard of somebody who'd had four replacements, and by the time I had to have my third, I figured they'd know how to get blood out with a laser beam or something.

I went back to the golf course. I went back to the streets, single after my third divorce. I went back to a normal workload.

And I went back to all my old habits, namely vodka and cigarettes. Drinking and smoking will kill you. So will getting run over by a truck. My greatest rationale for continuing my wanton ways was that I had been born with my heart problem; it hadn't been caused by lifestyle.

Plus, I'd already made up my mind to quit smoking once I turned forty. That gave me nine more months to smoke, so I ignored my quaking value, lit up another Marlboro, and had a drag.

I knew I could quit. I had quit once, and this isn't a joke. I quit smoking once for three years, from 1978 until 1981. I quit basically because I played tennis every day in those years, and I was losing a lot of third sets because the Marlboros would start calling.

Then I hurt my arm and couldn't play tennis anymore, so I started smoking again. Made perfect sense to me.

Does it say anywhere I ever claimed to be smart?

In October of '86, I had a great fortieth birthday. A friend named Loran Smith and his wife, Myrna, gave me a surprise party at their house in Athens after a Georgia football game in which an airplane had flown over Sanford Stadium carrying a banner that read, LORDY, LORDY, LEWIS GRIZZARD IS FORTY.

Friends from all parts of my life came, and I felt very special. I had a blind date with a wonderful young woman who defied what I considered to be all feminine tendencies and was a good sport about the whole thing, even about the fact that she was among strangers and I was too busy being very special to pay her much attention. We would be together for a time.

I didn't quit smoking, by the way. So sue me.

In the next several years, I bought a new house, a convertible, and my girlfriend even gave me a pair of white Gucci loafers I'd seen on a man at a golf tournament once and had lusted for afterward. I was on *The Tonight Show* a couple of times and, though I was nervous as hell, Johnny had complimented me on the laughs I'd gotten. I had some books on the *New York Times* best-seller list, too, despite the fact I'm a white Southern conservative male heterosexual. I'd even gotten the courage to leave the country again and went sailing around the Greek Isles. I had a hole-in-one and learned to play a decent hand of gin rummy after my rather expensive apprenticeship at the Ansley Golf Club in Atlanta was finally over.

I played poker occasionally, too. There was a group of us who got together maybe once a month for a game that was mostly a high-low, split-the-pot thing. I'll get back to that shortly.

Naturally, I did have to make occasional visits

back to the doctor for checkups. There is one truth about valve replacements. No matter what sort of artificial valve is implanted, there always will be a leak. Medical science has not found a way to fit a perfect artificial value into a patient.

And because I had to return to my doctor, I also had to have further blood work done. At least my veins had time to heal between visits, and I didn't have to become violent with any bloodsuckers. Life was good. But then came that phone call.

We were playing poker at my house. There were maybe eight of us. It was around ten in the evening. I had been to my longtime doctor a few days earlier. It is the practice of my physician to call his patients at home with the results of an examination. I have a very good, dedicated physician, Dr. Thorne Winter of Atlanta.

The phone rang. I was holding a seven-four low. It looked like a lock for half a fairly good pot.

Somebody who had dropped out of the hand answered the phone.

"It's your doctor," he said.

I put down my hand and went into my office to take the call.

There were some problems with my blood, Dr. Winter said. My count was down. The red blood cells seemed to be taking a beating.

I made the mistake of asking what could be causing all this.

"Could be a number of things," said my doctor.

"For instance?" I went on.

"Hepatitis," he began. "AIDS, or maybe a tumor

in your liver. You'll need to come back for more blood studies."

I went back upstairs, lost the hand to a perfect five-low, ran everybody out, and went to bed and cried.

"Goddammit all to hell."

Those were my very words.

I go through two heart surgeries, live through them both, and now I'm being told I could have hepatitis, AIDS, or a tumor in my liver.

The sledgehammer just hit, the realization that immortality was somehow slipping away with the zip on your fastball. I was old enough to die. The great shield of youth was gone. I could hear the doctor's words:

"You should think about getting your affairs in order."

You panic is what you do in a situation like that. Or at least that's what I did. I panicked, got out of bed, got drunk, and stayed up all night calling people telling them how I was going to die. I continued to cry through most of that, and I threw a couple of glasses against the wall between calls. I screamed at God a few times, too, and beat the walls with my fists. I was a mess by morning when I had to decide how to deal with yet another health crisis. At least I'd known about the heart. It had been diagnosed when I was fifteen. But this blindsided me.

I wanted my mother. She was an invalid by that time. I called my girlfriend. She came over and made certain I got a shower and a shave. She made breakfast and drove me to the doctor.

In the next month, I had 1,416 tests. I know that sounds like a lot, but I counted them. You name a test, and I had the sucker. Kodak stock went up eight points on the film they used to make pictures of my innards. Before many of these tests, I had to drink certain liquids, like iodine, barium, Pennzoil, dishwater, python sweat, and goat urine, which tasted better than any of the rest of it.

And, oh, did the blood flow again.

"You're severely anemic," my doctor said one day.

"You would be, too," I replied. "if somebody had a needle in your arm sucking out your blood every five goddamn minutes."

My mouth had turned trashy, too. It was the goat urine.

The cancer test was the scariest one—the test to find out whether or not I had a tumor in my liver, which was fouling up my blood. Before I could take it, I had to sign one of those releases that said, in small print, that I could die from the test. That will make your day.

"Let me hold the release while I'm taking the test," I said to the nurse, Miss G. Reaper, who gave me the release.

"Why?" she asked.

"Because," I explained, "if I feel like I'm going to die at any point during this test, I'm going to eat the release so you can't prove I ever signed it."

She wouldn't give me the release.

I had to sit in an examining room in my doctor's office for forty-five minutes, alone, waiting for the results of the test to come up to him. I'm not talking about a waiting room. Everybody has waited in a doctor's waiting room. That's another thing they teach in medical school:

"Make 'em wait as long as you can in the waiting room, so they won't have as much energy left in case you have to stick a tube into a sensitive place."

The thing about waiting in an examining room is, the nurse has brought in your file and placed it on a table, and you have this tremendous urge to open it and read it. Only you're not certain if that's against the rules or not.

When you were a kid, and they summoned you to the principal's office, they always put your *permanent record* on the desk in front of you as you waited for the principal. Your permanent record is the one that says whether or not you deserve the right to live and prosper in a free country after you are out of high school.

As soon as you are out, a copy is sent to every college and place of employment in the world, so if you are a worthless little pissant, as your coaches suggested on many occasions, they will know about it and won't allow you in school or give you a job.

You did something like chew gum in class when I was in high school, and Miss McGuire would say, "Give me that gum! This is going on your permanent record."

So there you sit in the principal's office, and you obviously have this urge to look and see if Miss McGuire did put the gum-chewing incident in there and if your record is marked *"Not Suitable Under Any Conditions."*

But you know better than to do that, because if you were caught, that would go on your permanent record, too.

"This person was caught looking at his permanent record when the principal wasn't in the room. He not only shouldn't be allowed in college or given a job, he should be shot on sight."

But what's the rule in a doctor's examining office? You're not some sniveling teenager. You are a grown-up. What could anybody do to you if you were caught going through your own medical file? Stick a needle in your arm and draw out some of your blood? Stick a large rod up your butt? They're probably going to do that anyway, whether you look at your file or not.

My file was sitting on the table as I waited for the results of my cancer test. I hesitated at first.

Then I thought, Here I sit waiting for the results of my cancer test, and I'm hesitating as to whether or not I'm going to look at my medical file.

I opened it. An alarm went off. A red light in the ceiling started blinking. The door burst open, and there stood Miss McGuire, my former homeroom teacher.

"You're not looking at your file, are you?" she asked.

"No ma'am," I assured her.

"Well, you'd better not be," she said, "or you're going straight to the principal's office, where Coach Leatherhead is going to put a needle in your arm and draw out your blood."

I don't know about anybody else, but I tend to

hallucinate in an examining room while waiting for results of a cancer test.

I never did attempt to open my file. My hands were shaking too much anyway. I'd been through the heart thing twice, but they had proved they could mend my heart. But cancer? A tumor in my liver? I had already asked my doctor, a cardiologist and internist, what the prognosis would be if such a thing were found.

He put it in sporting terms for me:

"That would pretty much be the ball game."

Naturally, I had considered I might die before my first heart operation. But I knew the number of such procedures they do these days and what a brilliant success rate has been achieved, so, had I been asked to wager my testicles on living and dying, I would have gone with living. Before the second operation, I was too sick and delirious to even know I had testicles, so it hadn't really been a concern.

But here I sat, perhaps about to hear those awful words, "Three months, tops," which was not the answer to the question. "How much longer could the pro basketball season really last?"

I prayed.

I shook.

I prayed some more.

Oddly, an old joke came into my mind:

A man was sitting next to a priest at a boxing match. Before the bell rang for the first round, one of the boxers crossed himself. "Will that help him,

Father?" asked the man. "Not if he can't fight," said the priest.

I prayed some more. It certainly couldn't hurt.

My doctor walked into the examining room and said, "The tests are fine."

I didn't have cancer. Want a thrill? Have a doctor order a test to find out whether or not you have a cancer and then have the test turn up the fact that you don't. It's like having every dinosaur in *Jurassic Park* lifted right off your Olds van. It was like winning in the ninth or hitting the lottery. It was Kim Basinger slipping off her bra and telling you to call the front desk for a wake-up call the next morning. It was salvation and deliverance and finding out your girlfriend really wasn't pregnant back in 1962.

It was twice as good as any of that.

Dr. Winter did bring me back within a light-year or two of earth by reminding me I still had the blood problem. Other tests had ruled out the hepatitis possibility, and I had dodged the AIDS bullet as well. I had had two heart operations, of course, and many blood transfusions. So when the HIV test had come back negative, the relief I felt rivaled that of the cancer miss.

"That's all I need," I had said to friends, who often noted my weight loss with skeptical, worried eyebrows. "To get through all I've been through and then come up with AIDS from blood transfusions."

I said the following in an earlier book and was roundly chastised by a critic who despised the work, but I'll say it again:

I knew damn well if I did turn out to have AIDS from the transfusions, many would note, "I knew that son of a bitch was queer."

We homophobes and Rush Limbaugh fans do suffer from such fears. So sue us.

There were more tests. And more weight loss. I dropped down from 185 to 160. My stamina didn't seem to be that lacking, but I did notice dull, aching pains in my upper legs when I walked up steps or climbed a hill on a golf course.

And there was my color. I didn't notice color. I was still playing a lot of golf and thought I simply had a nice tan. As a matter of face, it was the Monday after a member-guest tournament at my club in Atlanta when two friends, both notorious drinkers, made a conference call to my house.

"We need to talk to you," one said.

"So talk," I said.

"I didn't like your color at the member-guest party Saturday night," one went on.

"The red shirt didn't go with the green-and-yellow pants?"

"The color of your skin. You looked yellow. You're drinking too much."

It didn't end there. A man I love very much and have known for many years picked me up for dinner one evening in his hometown. After dinner he was supposed to take me to the airport so I could catch a flight home.

"You're jaundiced," he said in the car, "you've got to have help now."

He was ready to board a plane with me at that moment for a trip to the Betty Ford Center.

I would have none of it.

I did not try to argue with anybody that I wasn't an alcoholic. Of course I am. I once was standing outside a college auditorium about to go in to give a speech. There was a poster outside that asked ten questions:

"Answer five of these 'yes,' " said the sign, "and you could have a drinking problem."

I answered *all* of them "yes."

Yes, I drank to forget (I also drank to remember, however). Yes, I drank because it made me more comfortable in social situations (and cuter, too). Yes, I often drank to excess (and either said to hell with dinner or slept through it).

And then there was the part about an alcoholic parent, my father.

But I had the classic stubbornness of the alcoholic. In the immortal words of an older friend of mine, who said he'd been drinking professionally for nearly sixty years, "Nobody messes with my drinking."

The doctors had tried, of course. I was always having this conversation with a doctor:

"How about your drinking?"

"What do you mean?"

"How much are you drinking?"

"I'm not sure."

"An ounce a day?"

"Probably more than that."

"Two?"

"More than that."

"Three?"

"Keep going."

I didn't know how many ounces of alcohol I was drinking a day. I did drink most every day, I certainly admit that. And I enjoyed it. It was a little reward I often gave myself when my work was done.

Plus, I said to everybody else and myself, "I never drink until my work is done."

That was true. Mostly. There were times, however, I was supposed to make a speech at eight o'clock and never got on until ten and made up the two hours in the hotel bar.

I used to say, "I was a funny son of a bitch at eight, but I've been in the bar for two hours waiting on you folks to finish eating."

Nobody ever asked for their money back. That, I know.

The one thing I have never done, however, is write a column while drinking. The reason for that is quite simple:

I can really think of funny stuff when I'm drinking, but I can't get it down on a piece of paper because I can't type drunk. Just can't do it. It all comes out, "X##%!KYdd, mr-p, dq."

I drank only beer and an occasional glass of wine until 1980, when I also became an insomniac. That happened because I had a lot to do and couldn't cut my mind off at night. Then I began to drink vodka. Drinking vodka put me to sleep.

Insomnia can kill, too, I'm convinced of that. In-

somnia made me an angry person. It had a lot to
do with another failed marriage, as well as a lot
to do with my increased drinking. You toss around
in that bed and stare at that ceiling long enough,
and the frustration and the desperation become almost unbearable. To my own credit, I did finally
seek some medical help in that area, prior to my
second heart surgery. I was placed on a mild dose of
an antidepressant, which did, in fact, improve my
sleeping, especially if I had some vodka with it.
What was worse, or better, is the medicine also
kept me from having hangovers the next morning.

My friends began to hate me. They all felt like
hell the next day, and I didn't.

What they never understood is that a few drinks
on top of those pills made me sleepy, so I was
asleep by ten o'clock, while they stayed up and continued drinking. I gave up late nights for decent
sleep.

I actually was drinking less as a result.

But all of a sudden I was into pills and booze,
and then came the weight loss and the anemia and
the fact everybody said I looked yellow, and damn,
did I have to fight off the Lifestyle Police at every
turn. Friends counseled and held meetings without
me and called my doctors anonymously to tell them
I was drinking myself to death. These were all one
of three sorts of individuals:

1. Recovered alcoholics. They want you to go to the
   next meeting with them.

2. Heavy drinkers themselves. They want *you* to quit drinking.
3. People who have never drunk at all. I disliked their meddling the most. What the hell did they know?

But I held forth against them all. I did what every sensible alcoholic would do in my situation. I ignored their pleadings and quit hanging around them. Luckily, there were enough other people who didn't give me any crap, so I began spending more time with them.

I must admit, however, I did make one change in my drinking habits. I drank screwdrivers—vodka and orange juice. But I liked the taste of vodka more than I liked the taste of orange juice, and bartenders inevitably put, for my taste, too much orange juice in a screwdriver. What I did was start ordering double vodkas in a tall glass. Then I would order a glass of orange juice—with no ice in it—on the side. That way, I could put the amount of orange juice I wanted in my drink to suit my taste.

These became known, in places I haunted, as "Double Grizzards" or "Good Night, Lewis." Four usually sent me to bed quite happy.

I must mention one other factor that was contributing to my drinking, and please keep in mind here that I am not offering excuses. I'm just trying to explain.

I don't like to fly. I was absolutely terrified of it in an earlier period of my life. I was afraid my plane would crash, and I would burn and die. That is the thing that has always frightened me the most.

But I had to make a key decision in my life in the early 1980s. Opportunities to travel and to make a great deal of money—speaking engagements—were increasing incredibly. To take advantage, I had to fly, and I had to fly a lot. One day, before a flight from Atlanta's Hartsfield Airport, I went to the Delta Crown Room and drank lots of vodka.

The subsequent flight was the best I ever had. I wasn't nervous at all. I didn't have to listen to the sounds of the engines closely in order to know whether or not there had been any changes, indicating perhaps a loss of oil or the fact that large birds were being ground up in them. I read once where there had been an air crash because a bunch of birds were sucked into the engines.

I didn't have to watch the wings to make sure one hadn't fallen off. I didn't have to watch for sudden changes of expressions on the faces of the flight attendants. You see a flight attendant go from a happy face to a frown, and you know the captain has just informed her to get everyone in crash position because he's just flown through a swarm of late condors.

I took this thing as far as I could. I would have a couple of drinks on the way to the airport, and then however many I could down in the Crown Room before the flight; then I would beg a couple more while we were still on the ground to get me through the hurtling down the runway and leaping into the sky, something that still doesn't make sense to me, as in, how can anything as big and heavy as an airplane get off the ground?

Then I would drink while the flight was taking place until sleep overtook me. I was rarely awake during any landings, which I hated anyway. And one other thing about drinking on an airplane: Why do they take away your drink during takeoffs and landings? That's when I always needed one the most.

Thanks to alcohol, I was comfortable on airplanes for the first time in my life. I actually began to look forward to flying. I could get drunk as Cooter Brown, and usually there was nobody around to tell the pilot to head the plane toward Betty Ford.

The only problem any of this caused was, I often wasn't a very pretty sight coming off an airplane, thus, I had to schedule flights the evening before any sort of activity was to take place. I also always managed to have a trustworthy person along on the flight with me to make certain I got from the airport safely into my hotel room, where I was promptly locked in. Employees and friends both served in this capacity.

I didn't have hepatitis. I didn't have AIDS. I didn't have cancer. My liver function wasn't the best it could have been, but I continued to blame all that on the blood, which my doctor agreed certainly was at least a part of it, despite the fact he continued to badger me about my drinking.

But after more tests, he was finally sure what was, in fact, causing the low blood count and the destruction of the red blood cells. He had had his suspicions, but Dr. Thorne Winter is a thorough man, and he had wanted to make certain he was making the proper diagnosis, for the cancer, AIDS, hepatitis scares.

It was the second valve.

It was 1990. The second valve, attached in that emergency situation, in an effort to save my life as I battled the infection, was leaking badly again, and, it was explained to me, an outer ring had to be attached to my aorta to have something on which to attach the valve. That's how large an opening had been left in the aorta due to what the infection had destroyed.

The blood was hitting this ring, and its various ingredients were being scattered throughout my body, a lot of it going to my liver.

"Your body is producing plenty of blood," I was told, "but it's being destroyed, and the other organs are having problems handling all the garbage they're getting from the breakup."

I knew better than to ask, but I asked anyway.

"Well, doctor," I said to Thorne Winter, "what can be done about it?"

"You're going to have to have another valve."

A football coach once said to me, about winning and losing, "The highs are never as high as the lows are low."

What an incredible high finding out I didn't have cancer. What a piercing low finding out about a possible third valve replacement, and I use the word "possible" because, at that very moment, I wasn't certain I would ever consent to another.

Goddammit, I'd had two—what was the deal here? You couldn't just keep splitting open a man's chest and gouging around in his heart.

I could have eaten nails. Chewed aluminum siding. Caught an elephant and killed it with my bare hands and ate the son of a goddamn bitch, to quote a guy with whom I used to play tennis.

Whenever a patient is diagnosed by one doctor, I had already learned, he or she will insist upon sending you to other doctors for further opinions and further tests. I'm not certain if doctors don't necessarily trust their own opinions, or if they have dealt with other doctors who go, "If I get somebody really screwed up, I'll send him over so you can take a look, too."

And I definitely was really screwed up. I had more vodka.

I also went to see a new doctor, Randolph Martin, head of noninvasive surgery at Emory. My kind of surgery. Dr. Martin was to give me a new kind of test. I thought I'd had them all by now.

Dr. Randolph Martin gave me a transesophageal echocardiagram. This is noninvasive surgery? You sign a release. You get a mild sedative—just enough to make you certain this is going to do more than sting a little. Then somebody brings in a tube. Everybody's got some kind of tube in a hospital. When you have heart surgery, they put tubes in every orifice, not to mention in places there previously had not been an orifice until somebody made one.

But this tube was different. You have to swallow

this tube. That is exactly what I said, and that is exactly what I meant. You have to *swallow* this tube.

I gag on a large pinto bean, and here a man is asking me to swallow a tube that then goes down my esophagus and gives doctors a look at the back of my heart.

"I'm sure it looks a lot like the front of my heart," I said as I stared at the tube.

But you get a doctor with the opportunity to do a procedure involving a tube, and he won't be stopped.

You know how hard it is to swallow a tube? Don't try it, of course, but go outside and look at your garden hose and think about taking it right on down your gullet. I'm not saying this tube was the size of a garden hose, but it wasn't a strand of angel-hair pasta, either.

They put the tube in my mouth. They pushed it toward my tonsils.

I coughed. I gagged. I resisted that tube going down my throat with all I had in me. I would have resisted by punching a few people out, but somebody had my arms.

They put the tube in my mouth again. Same result.

Third time, they took it deeper than before, and this was worse than anything a dentist had ever tried to do to me.

I swallowed the tube. Once a tube is shoved that deeply into your throat, I found out, reflex action takes place, and you swallow. During heart surgery, a respirator is put in the patient's throat, but the patient is asleep at the time. They gave me some reason they couldn't put me to sleep for this. I think it had to do with the fact it wasn't as much fun for the student assistants if the patients were asleep.

The transesophageal said the same thing all the other tests said: Yes, the valve was leaking. Yes, the ring was tearing up my blood. Yes, I'd have to have the third surgery.

"It's a matter of when," said Dr. Martin, who, despite the fact that he had ordered such a thing to be done to me, turned out to be a warm, understanding man who seemed to have a notion of just how much I wanted to stay away from a third surgery as long as I possibly could. I wanted to put it off until just after Christmas 2055.

"First," he explained, "you don't want to wait until the heart becomes too enlarged from having to pump harder. There is the point where it will not return to its previous size. It's like stretching a rubber band so far and so long that it will not regain its size and elasticity.

"Secondly, you had a hard time in your second operation. You don't want to wait until a third is also an emergency.

"Thirdly, your blood is really being trashed, and that is making it tough on your other organs.

"And, fourthly, I don't like the way you look."

He mentioned my color, my thinness, the fact that I looked tired, and the fact that my nail beds were pale. I wondered what that had to do with anything.

"Look at mine," he said.

They were pink.

"Now, look at yours."

They were chalk-colored. The anemia.

I had a question:

"What about a third surgery?" I asked. "What would be my chances?"

"There will be a lot of scar tissue left from the other two operations," he answered. "That means there will be a lot of bleeding. But there are ways to control that. I can't guarantee anything, of course, but my gut reaction is you would do fine."

But wasn't there some doubt in his voice somewhere? Scar tissue. That meant it would be harder for the surgeon to find places on which to set good sutures to assure the valve stayed in place. It seemed to me there was a decent chance I could bleed to death, plus there would be more transfusions and another run at AIDS.

Would this ever end? Would there ever again be a time in my life I was free from fear and concern about my health? I went back to an old crutch:

If I hadn't had this thing, I retold myself, *I would have been drafted in 1968, never received a medical deferment, and, six months later, somebody named Ding Dong Dang would have put one right between my eyes in a rice paddy. It could have saved my life.*

That lasted me about eight seconds before I felt the rage return.

I shuffled out of Dr. Martin's Emory Hospital office angry, gaunt, tired, yellow, with chalky nail beds.

I tried to ignore all this at first. The old denial process. The doctor had said it was a matter of when, so I could wait awhile. Who knows? Maybe I could wait ten years. Or even fifteen.

I was in a hotel bar with friends. One of my friends had a date along. We got into the booze rather heavily, and the conversation got around to faith healing. You get enough booze involved, and conversations can get around to almost anything.

My friend's date, drunk as a goat, suddenly said, "I once helped other people at my church lay hands on one of our members who had cancer, and he recovered completely. It was a miracle."

What had she said?

"I said, 'He recovered completely.' It was a miracle."

Right there in that bar—and I was serious as a barium enema—I had her lay her hands on my chest and see if she could chase the devil that lurked inside my heart.

The manager of the bar thought we were about to engage in some sick sexual perversion or were involved in the occult, so he kicked us out. In retrospect, hard to blame him.

I remained hopeful the woman had helped me until my friend told me she left the church and had gone to work for the American Civil Liberties Union.

I managed to tap-dance around this thing for three more years. I went back to Dr. Martin's office.

And back. And back again. And again. More blood work. More echocardiagrams. No more tube swallowing, however. I had threatened numerous lives if the subject even came up again.

Each time it was the same.

"The problem is there. It won't ever go away. Don't put if off too long."

★★★ 4 ★★★

D<small>R. MARTIN CALLED THE MEETING. HE WANTED ME</small> there, of course, along with Dr. Ellis Jones, who performed my first two surgeries. The purpose of the meeting was to set the exact date for my third surgery.

We met on February 3, 1993, at Dr. Martin's office at Emory. Driving over, I remembered the meeting I had had with Dr. Willis Hurst, my cardiologist, to schedule my first surgery. The decision had been made to put in a pig valve.

"Let me ask you this," I said to Dr. Hurst after the date was set—March 22, 1982. "I'm thirty-five. I would like to live to be around seventy-five. Will this valve last me that long?"

"Let me ask you this," Dr. Hurst had replied. "How many forty-year-old hogs do you know?"

We met, doctors Martin and Jones and myself, in one of the examining rooms. I was in the middle. Dr. Jones was to my left, Dr. Martin to my right. I think doctors always find a way to get you in the middle. Regardless of which way you run, one will have a shot at stopping you.

We went over each other's schedules. I had a couple of speeches coming up. Dr. Jones had a medical conference in a couple of weeks. Dr. Martin had to go to one, too.

We agreed the surgery would be March 22. I didn't note at the time that that would be the exact anniversary of my first heart surgery.

I again expressed my concern about the scar tissue.

"There will be some bleeding," said Dr. Jones, "but we can handle that."

"There are some new experimental drugs we can use if we have to," Dr. Martin added.

Experimental drugs.

"Just don't let me die, guys," I said, as cavalierly as I could, which wasn't all that cavalierly.

"You aren't going to die," said Dr. Jones with assurance.

But then I remembered that surgeons are a lot like test pilots, full of confidence. Hell, yeah, I can fly that sucker.

But, nah, these guys wouldn't let me die. I must have said that to myself a million times during the following one-and-a-half months.

"And y'all both think the mechanical valve is the way to go?"

"No question," said Dr. Jones.

Dr. Martin agreed.

Mechanical valves last longer than pig valves. Nobody in that room—especially me, but the doctors, too—even wanted to think about the possibility of a fourth surgery.

Then Dr. Jones said this:

"Look, you're an old fart now. You're not running around in the woods anymore. You're a golfer. You don't live as active a life as you did before. So we need to do the definitive valve-replacement surgery on you. We'll take out that pig valve and put in a St. Jude's mechanical. You'll be chipping and putting again in about seven weeks."

I understood exactly what he was talking about. With a mechanical valve, it would be necessary for me to take a blood-thinning agent called Coumadin every day for the rest of my life. The thinner the blood, the less chance there is of a clot forming on one of the leaflets of the mechanical valve.

Also, however, the thinner the blood, the greater chance there is of bleeding to death if you sustain a nasty gash doing something in the out-of-doors like camping or running white water, which I certainly did at one point in my life.

But did he just call me an "old fart"? I think he did! I hadn't given up camping and running white water, which I had done for nearly fifteen years, because I had become an old fart and was too feeble to continue. I gave it up because the man who introduced me to it, my friend Browny Stephens, had died, and it just wasn't the same without him. I also gave it up because Browny always put up the tent, and I never learned how.

I certainly didn't think Dr. Jones was trying to be derisive when he called me an old fart. Of course, even if he had been, you don't go messing with somebody who knows his way around a scalpel. But on the way home, I decided to give this old-fart thing a little more thought.

Okay, I got out of college in 1968. I was twenty-one in 1968. This was 1993. So, I subtracted sixty-eight from ninety-three and got fifteen and added that to twenty-one. That made me thirty-six. Right? Right. I was thirty-six.

You're not an old fart when you're thirty-six. You're an old fart when you'd rather play bingo than hit the neon in search of the pleasures of the night.

You're an old fart when you spend more time on park benches feeding a bunch of pigeons than you do thinking about whether you've finally got enough money to buy a red Jaguar convertible.

Old farts buy Winnebagos and get rates at Best Westerns. They can get that cheap insurance some over-the-hill celebrity is selling on television. Old farts have trouble going to the bathroom, they wear silly-looking straw hats, they breathe with their mouths open, and they drive eleven miles an hour in the passing lane on the interstate. And they shrink.

I swear that old farts shrink. The older they get,

the more they shrink. They get smaller and smaller, and when they drive eleven miles an hour in the passing lane of the interstate, they can barely see over the steering wheel.

I'm not an old fart. I by God have a red Jaguar convertible, and I still stand a full six-one, and I don't own a straw hat, silly-looking or otherwise. My bowels are so regular, the Naval Observatory sometimes calls me just to make sure what time it is.

I can't remember where I was when the Japs attacked Pearl Harbor or where I was when the news came FDR had died in Warm Springs, Georgia. The reason is, I wasn't even born when those things happened.

Except for that little matter about my heart, I'm still 160 pounds of lean, mean machine.

All right. So there have been a few subtle changes that might indicate I'll be an old fart one day. But not today. As long as I can convince myself sixty-eight from ninety-three is fifteen, I'm in business.

Subtle changes. One is women and girls under twenty-five have started calling me "mister." Another is that I have hair protruding out of a few telltale places such as my nose and ears.

I guess hair has always grown in my nose; it's just never gotten long enough to see until a few years ago. As far as ear hair goes, I didn't know there was any such thing (except for that little fuzz on your lobes) until recently. But sure enough, all of a sudden, I've got hair growing out of my ears, too.

I met a young girl in a bar and asked her to dance. She replied, "Sorry, mister, but I don't dance with men who have hair growing out of their nose and ears."

After that, I went out and bought myself a pair of small scissors to keep my nose and ear hair trimmed. I have to do it about twice a week. I met another young woman in a bar soon after I began trimming my various new hairs. I asked her to dance, and she replied, "I know you, mister. You and my daddy were in college together."

Still, staying with the hair theme, I'm not gray-headed. I do have an occasional gray hair in my head, but I've never even had to price any of those hair-coloring agents. I've still got *all* my hair, too.

I've got a nice thick head of hair. When women older than twenty-five run their fingers through it, they say things like, "Oooo, Lewis." Once a woman did that, and then she said, "Oooo, Lewis. You've really got a bad dandruff problem." I'd quit using the Pine-Sol after my third divorce.

But I solved that, too. I went out and bought some of that shampoo that smells like Pine-Sol. You've seen it advertised on television. A guy is standing in the shower, and his head is covered neatly with that shampoo. I've always wondered how you got shampoo lather to sit up on your head without dripping or running into your eyes, but what do I know about the shampoo industry?

Anyway, I put some of that stuff on my head as I stood in the shower. Just then, a camera crew burst into my bathroom, threw my shower door open, and, without thinking, I shouted, "It's working! I can actually *feel* it working!"

I haven't had a problem with dandruff since.

The tape of my taking a shower with shampoo that smells like Pine-Sol will be part of an upcoming segment of *Hard Copy* entitled "Why Did God Make Men's Bodies So Ugly?"

There is my beard, however. When I was in my late twenties, somebody told me I had a weak chin, and that's why women wouldn't dance with me. So, in order to cover it up, I grew myself a beard. I still had trouble getting a dance with a strange woman, but at least little children who saw me didn't tug on their mother's skirts anymore and say, "Mommy, look at that man with no chin."

The beard went fine for a while. Then it slowly began to turn gray right around my chin area. I thought God was punishing me for trying to cover up His mistake, giving me a weak chin.

The gray began to spread. A year later, my beard was almost completely gray. A woman I asked to dance said she was a history major and could she interview me on my experiences in World War I for a thesis she was writing.

I shaved the beard off. I still have that weak chin, but I've been working on it in the gym. They have this small barbell for people like me. You strap it on your chin and nod up and down for fifty reps. They say I will be able to see some definition in my chin any day now.

As far as my lifestyle goes, it's hardly sedentary. I mentioned I don't pigeon-feed from a park bench. I

certainly don't sit and rock and doze off and drool. I
also don't play bingo, and I don't have any grandchildren.

I live quite an active life, thank you. I play golf
practically every day the sun shines. And I don't
hit from the senior tees. Although I do have a heart
condition, I don't whine and beg for those flags for
my golf cart that allow me to drive on the course
when it's wet and everybody else has to stay on the
cart paths.

I've had a hole-in-one, and I shot a par 71, with
five birdies, once at the Greensboro, North Carolina, Country Club. I am a past winner of both the
member-member and the member-guest tourna-
ments at the Melrose Club on Daufuskie Island,
South Carolina, and I once had back-to-back net
eagles playing in a pro-am with Greg Norman,
thank you very much.

I've never had an American Association of Retired Persons card so I could get rates at motels, either, and I still occasionally watch dirty movies in
my hotel rooms when they have Spectravision.
Once I saw three in one night, *Talk Dirty to Me*,
Talk Dirty to Me, II, and *Debbie Does Dallas for the
Sixteenth Time*.

I might be a lot of things, I thought to myself,
but I'm not an old fart. Not yet.

That conclusion lasted until the evening news,
and they were talking about something brand-new
President Bill Clinton had goofed on.

That's when it hit me. Sixty-eight from ninety-
three isn't fifteen at all. It's twenty-five. And

twenty-five and twenty-one is forty-six, and that's
how old I was, and that's how old the president of
the United States was, too.

My God. Not only was I about to have my third
heart surgery and could die, *I WAS THE SAME
AGE AS THE PRESIDENT OF THE UNITED
STATES.*

God help me. I felt a sudden shortage of breath.
No wonder I had ear hair.

Presidents are *old* guys like Ronald Reagan and
Harry Truman and Martin Van Buren, my favorite
president. I don't think Martin Van Buren did anything while he was president, and I think that's the
way it should be.

The realization frightened and startled me, because if I am as old as the president, then I might,
in fact, truly be an old fart.

I recovered for a moment when I realized that
for damned sure I was not mature or responsible
enough to be president. But that feeling of well-
being disappeared when I realized, well, what's so
different about Bill Clinton? He doesn't strike me
as the most mature guy in the world. And then another realization came over me:

The Clinton campaign talked about "change,"
talked about "a new generation taking charge."

And that's just what happened, wasn't it? Good-
bye, old soldier. Hello, baby boomer. Mine and Bill
Clinton's baby-boomer class was the very first.
Nineteen hundred and forty-six. The soldiers had
just come home, and the bedsprings of a nation
awakened. Our parents mass-produced us.

We became the chosen ones. The young and, yes, the restless, if you will, in so many ways. We were the first generation to grow up with television. We drove cars to and from high school. We went to college en masse. Some of us tried to burn down our colleges over Vietnam. Elvis belonged to us. Rock and roll belonged to us. We became a zillion—at least—lawyers. We became bankers and real estate tycoons, and politicians, and drug dealers, and journalists. We saw journalists bring down a president.

And we would be forever young, wouldn't we? We would have the energy and the money to do all the things our parents never got a chance to do. The ride would never end. We would laugh and love, and nothing would ever slow us down.

But look at us now. The class of '46 has a man in the White House, and I'm about to have my third heart surgery.

We're no longer promising young men. Our promise is behind us. We're in the midst of either fulfilling it or failing now.

The surgeon was right. I *am* an old fart. I guess I can tell the truth now. Besides those subtle changes, my eyes don't work like they used to. I mentioned my sleeping problems, and often I awaken with a stiff back. As another old-fart friend of mine said, trying to loosen up on the golf course one day, "Damn, everything's still stiff about me but the right thing."

Meanwhile, I had one-and-a-half months before the surgery to do a lot of thinking, which I did. I kept thinking, Son of a bitch, this damn thing gets closer every day.

I also thought a lot about how all this had happened to me. Why me? Why in the hell did I have to come into this world forty-six years ago with a bad aortic valve?

I wondered if something had happened at the moment of my conception that might have caused all this. I should have asked my mother while she was still alive.

It's something I think everybody would be interested in. Were you conceived after an evening at an Italian restaurant where a strolling accordionist sang, "Come Back to Sorrento," *"Arrivederci, Roma,"* or *"Al Di La"?* Did a bottle or two of a Valpolicella induce the romance that followed after the dinner? Or had your old man been out drinking beer and came home randy because he'd been able to pick up an elusive 7–10 split?

I did come up with one possible theory about my conception and what went wrong enough to cause my faulty valve.

My mother met my father at the Terminal Railroad Station in Atlanta when he came back from Europe and World War II. Then they boarded the Man-o'-War passenger train for Columbus, Georgia, home of Fort Benning, where Daddy was stationed after the war and where I was born. That's fact. The next is only conjecture.

Perhaps during the three-hour train ride between Atlanta and Columbus my parents, separated for three years, had become amorous and had found a way and at that moment, that key moment, the train had hit a bump, causing my problem.

Or perhaps my parents had been forced into cramped quarters, and my father hadn't been able to get a good toehold.

Regardless, when people ask me what sign I was born under, I do say, "I'm not certain, but it could have been the one that says, 'Dining car in the opposite direction.' "

Or, had my mother been frightened by something while she was carrying me? There was a kid in my school with a decidedly pointed head. My boyhood friend and idol Weyman C. Wannamaker, Jr., a great American, had once observed that perhaps that kid's mother had been scared by a pyramid during her pregnancy.

I am certain, however, I was born in the wee morning hours of October 20, 1946, at the base hospital in Fort Benning. That could have been my problem. At that hour, maybe the only person around to deliver me had been the dentist who would slap me several years later.

I also know I weighed five pounds—and change—and that I was a month premature. I also know two relatives said, when they first got a look at me, "There's something wrong with Christine's baby."

They later told me I was quite red of face, and, as one later explained to me, "You had one eye pointed toward Miami and the other toward Washington, D.C." I often ask myself what my eyes might have looked like in that condition.

I supposed if I had been facing east, my left eye would have been at our nation's capital and my right at Miami. If I had been shaded toward the west, then it would have been the opposite. My eyeballs, in either case, would have been quite far apart. Maybe Daddy had been bowling that night. My eyes would have been at the exact position of the dreaded 7–10 split.

Regardless, I am happy to report my eyes finally did return to the point that when my left eye looked toward Miami or Washington, so did my right, and all the vices and versas that are involved here.

Something did turn out to be wrong with me, though. But this is something that still hurts to repeat:

My mother was in the hospital herself when I had my first operation. She suffered from a disease called scleroderma that would eventually kill her.

My cousin Mary Ann spent the day with her. She told me later that Mother said, time after time, "I hope I didn't do anything wrong to hurt Lewis."

I must have assured her a million times after that that she most certainly hadn't.

I continued to think in terms of family, though, in my search for a reason for my condition. Genetics.

Pat! I hadn't thought of her! Here I had already been through two heart surgeries, and I hadn't even thought of my second cousin, Pat Lee, who was one of the first people in the country to have open-heart surgery.

Pat's mother, Glenda, was my first cousin, the youngest of my maternal Aunt Jessie. I was seven when Pat was born. Mother and I were living in Moreland with my grandparents, next door to Aunt Jessie.

Pat was born in 1953 with a hole in her heart. It was a horrible family crisis. Without surgery, Pat would die.

In 1953, you didn't just drive thirty-five miles to Atlanta and Emory to have heart surgery. The procedure was in its infancy, and Pat would have to go for her operation to the Mayo Clinic in Rochester, Minnesota, where she would be placed on the amazing new contraption called the heart-lung machine that would do the work of the heart while surgeons worked.

I wouldn't have my first heart surgery for thirty years. Imagine the advances during that time.

Pat, her mother, and Aunt Jessie flew—the first flight for each of them—from Atlanta to Minnesota, where Pat was admitted to the Mayo Clinic.

The flight concerned everybody a great deal, especially my mother, who had flown her first and last time in an army hospital plane from Camp Chaffee, Arkansas, where my father was stationed in 1948, to Walter Reed Hospital in Washington.

She had come down with some mysterious disease that had weakened her terribly and had caused her to lose most of the hair on her head. Mother recovered, and luckily some of her hair grew back. There would always be a bald spot on the back of her head, however, which made her extremely self-conscious. She could cover it with other hair, but every time she went to the beauty parlor, she would worry, "Well, I guess I'm the only bald woman that ever goes in there."

Mama's airplane ride had lasted nearly twenty-four hours. The plane landed several times to pick up other patients before reaching Washington.

"I lay there on that cot," she would often say, "and was as scared as I've ever been. I never knew where we were or what was going to become of me, but I knew if I ever got off that thing, I'd never get on another one."

And she didn't, which is why the thought of Pat, Glenda, and Aunt Jessie flying upset her to no end.

"What if that thing was to fall?" I heard Mother say to my grandmother.

"Lord, Christine, don't even think of no such thing," my grandmother replied.

"But those things fall all the time," said my mother. "You just can't turn on the news or read the paper without seeing where another one has gone down."

Conversations like that eventually would lead to my own fear of flying.

Luckily, however, my Aunt Jessie is the trooper of the family. Her granddaughter was sick, and she would do anything, sacrifice anything, to see she got well.

"Lord, Jessie," Mother said to her, "I'm worried sick y'all's plane is not going to make it."

"Aw, Christine," Jessie said, "don't worry about

that. I remember you was even scared to ride Daddy's mule when you were a little girl."

We all could only imagine this place Pat and Glenda and Jessie were going to, this faraway place, as a world apart from our own. They were going to stop Pat's heart while the heart-lung machine kept her blood flowing. I cringed each time the situation was discussed, and my imagination ran wild.

I could see a doctor with a knife, slicing on little Pat's chest. Blood went everywhere. I knew nothing of anesthesia. I could hear Pat's screams of pain and fright and horror. That picture stayed with me into adulthood, too. Before my own first heart surgery, that horrid scene kept coming back to me. The mind of a child is a deep storage place.

In both Moreland churches—there was a Baptist and a Methodist—they prayed for the three brave ones among us who were about to go off on this journey into harm's way. I was a Methodist. Our preacher said, "Our heavenly Father, please be with this family in their time of danger and need."

I knew my mother, sitting next to me, was adding, "And don't let that plane fall."

The day they left, my mother came up with something else to worry about, perhaps to take her mind off the dreaded flight.

"I wonder what kind of scar little Pat's going to have?" she said after the family good-byes and Jessie's husband, Grover, had driven away for the trip to the airport.

I hadn't thought of the scar. Mother's mention of

it brought back the operating-room scene, and I could see little Pat with this big gash from her neck to her navel.

"I'd just hate to see that child have an ugly scar on her," Mother added. "She might have trouble finding a husband with something like that."

My mother was a worrier's worrier.

At Kitty Hawk, she would have said, "Poor Orville and Wilbur. What if they get that thing up, and it doesn't come down again?"

The flight to Mayo, the operation, and the flight back were all successes. Pat, Glenda, and Jessie were gone nearly a month. They had found a lady who rented them a small apartment. After today's heart surgeries, the patients are often released from the hospital inside a week.

Surgeons patched Pat's heart and sent her home, and Aunt Jessie said, upon arriving back in Moreland, "They were some fine people up there, but none of them know how to cook. I can't wait for some turnip greens and corn bread."

Pat is fine today. She now has children of her own, all healthy.

And the scar. Mother was gratified to see the surgeons had opened from side to side so that the scar would be hidden. Pat told her she could even wear a bathing suit without it being noticed.

"It's just that there's so many drownings these days," Mama said.

☞ ♥ ☜

So perhaps it had been genetics. Perhaps there was a connection between Pat and myself. I am happy to report, however, that as far as I know, there are currently no other members of the family having any heart problems.

In the last couple of weeks before D day, I basically decided not to sweat it. The vodka helped. What could I do about it, anyway, regardless of what had caused me to be facing another heart surgery? I found a little peace in that.

I checked my courage factor. It was still above normal. I prayed when I remembered to.

My golf game actually got a little better. Partners said, "You get this new valve, and you might gain some weight and get some more length off the tee."

That was a nice thought. I was sick of having to own one of the great short games of all time in order to make pars because I wasn't long enough off the tee to hit many greens in regulation.

What settled me in for the duration of the wait was recalling Chet Huntley, who, when dying of cancer, was asked why he thought he had been stricken by such a horrid fate.

"A roll of the dice," he had answered. "Just a roll of the dice."

✱✱✱ 5 ✱✱✱

THERE WERE STILL MORE TESTS TO RUN BEFORE I
checked into Emory for the surgery. Great.

The medical profession loves tests. Not only do
they make the medical profession a lot of money,
they're fun for the medical profession. If there is
pain and discomfort involved for the patient, that's
even more fun. I recall, before my first surgery, my
doctor ordering me a heart-catheterization test.
Said my doctor, "We just don't do heart surgery before we do a catheterization test."

That's because it's so much fun.

The patient lies down on a hard steel table. He is
wearing one of those thin robes with the back cut
out of it. Everybody else is fully clothed. The nurse

with the best sense of humor goes over to the thermostat and turns the temperature down.

"It's cold," says the patient, entering the room.

"You think you're cold now," says Judy Canova, the nurse, "wait until you lie down on the table."

As mentioned, the robe the patient is wearing has no back, and the table is made of steel. Remember that thing when you were a kid where you thought that if you licked a cold rail, your tongue would stick to it, and a train would come along and cut off your tongue?

It's the same thing with putting your butt on a cold steel table in a hospital. You might get stuck on the table, not be able to get off, and they'll practice sex-change operations on you.

You don't think this test is fun for a doctor? First he gets to cut a hole somewhere in your person— they cut one in my arm. Then they insert a tube into the hole and push it all the way up into your heart.

"There won't be any pain," the doctor says, almost regretfully. "There are no nerves in the heart."

I, frankly, wasn't worried about the pain. I had to sign another one of those releases before the test saying I realized all this could kill me. I was worried about this "killing me" part.

After the tube is in the heart, the doctor then shoots dye into the tube, which goes into the coronary arteries of the heart. The doctor can see what results on a small television screen above the table. He can see if any of the coronary arteries are blocked.

"You can look up and watch with me if you want to," the doctor said.

"If it's all the same to you," I replied, "I'll just keep my eyes closed and pray."

The doctor keeps shooting dye into the arteries and wiggles the catheter around, and when the dye leaves the coronary arteries, guess where it goes? Right to the bladder, that's where. Ever had to pee when you were a best man or maid of honor at a wedding? When you were camping out and the zipper on your sleeping bag was stuck? When you were sitting in a hopeless line of gridlocked freeway traffic? When your boss was telling you the story of how he got started in the aluminum-siding game?

That's how it is in heart catheterization. You have to pee unmercifully. Like a racehorse. You'd kill to pee.

But they don't dare let you get up off the table to go pee, and you don't particularly want to do that anyway, what with a strand of Mueller's spaghetti in your heart.

The nurse with the sense of humor runs water now and asks, "Have you ever been to Niagara Falls?" Then she says, "Surely, you can hold it a couple of more hours."

I held it for as long as I could, and then I threatened to kill somebody if I lived through the procedure, so they finally brought me a portable urinal for males, a bottle with a long neck on it.

It marked the first time I'd ever tried to pee lying flat on my back. The time I was stuck in my sleeping bag, I rolled over on my stomach and went right in the bag. It was the last night of the camping trip anyway. I had a much more difficult time trying to pee while lying flat on my back.

In fact, I found it nearly impossible. The frustration was awful. I had the desire and the receptacle. But I couldn't pull the trigger. I couldn't turn over on my stomach, either, with that wire in me and my coronary arteries on television.

Here's a tip if anything like this ever happens to you. Purely by chance, I happened to bend my knees up. I was chastised for moving, but with my knees up, I suddenly was able to relieve myself into that receptacle. The moment of purge remains one of the highlights of my life, as does the moment the doctor said, "That'll do it" and pulled the catheter out of me. It didn't hurt until the end got to the top of my right shoulder. From there on down to just above the middle of my arm, the location of the incision, it felt like he was removing my esophagus.

Tubes and catheters are like that, I have noticed. Coming out they are always bigger than when they went in, and they always hurt more. In show business, this is known as the big finale. In medicine, this is known as, It ain't over till it's over.

There wasn't time to do the catheterization before my second surgery. I was too close to dying. I begged not to have it before my third. In fact, I insisted I not have it. I went further than that. I said, "Anybody tries to catheterize me is going to be listening to the sounds of his anus with his stethoscope."

I refused to have a heart catheterization, in other words.

Both my surgeon, Dr. Jones, and my cardiologist, Dr. Martin, tried to talk me out of this decision, but they gave in when I mentioned the stethoscope thing and they saw my hands going for the dangling devices around their necks.

As an alternative, Dr. Martin mentioned something about some sort of test involving nuclear medicine. This didn't sound like anything I wanted to do, either. I recall Dr. No ordering the same sort of thing done to 007 once.

"Will there be any glowing involved in this?" I asked Dr. Martin.

He assured me there wouldn't be, but he mentioned there might be no-nuke protesters picketing outside the testing area.

"Be sure not to eat anything after midnight before the test," he explained, "and no coffee the next morning, either. You can have all the uranium you want to drink, however."

I'm still not certain what they did to me in this particular test. I do know I was marched into a room marked NUCLEAR MEDICINE, and a guy with colored hair and a sign that read JOHN 3:16 was standing outside the door. He said to me, "I had normal-colored hair before I went in there, too."

I was given an I.V., and a liquid was pumped into me. I heard the term "isotopes" being bandied about.

"This is Dr. Oppenheimer and Dr. Ferme," Dr.

Martin said to me. "They will be conducting the
test."

"What do you call this test?" I asked.

"We prefer to call it a project," said Dr. Oppenheimer.

"Manhattan or New England?" I wanted to know.

"Shhhh," interrupted Dr. Ferme. "This is top secret."

None of that happened, of course, but I think it
was a momentary illusion from the glass of uranium I had before bed.

After the I.V., I was asked to step up on the
stress-test machine. Somebody turned it on. I was
doing a fast walk. Sort of like I was trying to get to
a rest room in the Soviet Union before Mr. Bowel
Voice declared an emergency.

When I said I was completely exhausted (I lasted
about ten minutes, not bad for a man in my condition), I was instructed to step off the machine and
lie down on a table located next to it. Machines
whirred. Needles danced.

"Am I glowing?" I asked Dr. Martin.

"No," he answered, "but you're sweating like a
Clemson graduate trying to write a love letter."

I managed a chuckle. Then I noticed my left arm
had turned green.

"Don't worry about that," said Dr. Martin. "It's
just the light shining off Nurse Gilman's hair. One
too many isotopes."

The results of that test, I learned later, seemed
to indicate that I had no blocked arteries in my
heart, and it was okay to go ahead with the valve-

replacement surgery. I had nightmares for days about being locked in a room with a green-haired nurse named Enola Gay chasing me around with a samurai sword, but other than that, I had no after-effects from my first experience with nuclear medicine.

I received a letter from the doctor's office telling me to be at the hospital for check-in around noon on Sunday, March 21, and that my operation was scheduled at 7:00 A.M. the following morning.

Back in February, at my "old-fart" meeting with Dr. Jones and Dr. Martin, I had fully accepted the fact there would, indeed, be the third surgery. And I found myself fairly confident at this point, looking forward to getting the ordeal behind me, even trying to find a bright side to all this. I would feel better with the new valve, I decided. I wouldn't be anemic anymore. I wouldn't have bad color anymore. My nail beds would be pink again. I would have more energy.

But during the period when I was still trying to weasel my way out of the surgery, I'd had a great concern about the period leading up to the operation. Would I be able to sleep? Would I be depressed? Or a better question: *How* depressed would I be? I had even looked into some mood-altering drugs to use during the few weeks before the operation. Ultimately, the vodka and orange juice worked fine.

On the Wednesday before the surgery, friends gave the First and Last Pig Valve Invitational Golf Tournament on my behalf. Everybody got a golf

shirt with the name of the tourney written on it.
And get this: On the day before I entered the hospital, my golf club in Atlanta held a one-day
member-guest. My friend Tim Jarvis had flown in
from California to be with me during the surgery.
We entered the tournament and came in second,
missing victory by the slightest of margins.

My Sunday column, the last before the surgery,
wasn't a good-bye column. It was more of a see-you-
in-a-bit column. I asked readers to pray for me.

I had already canceled various appointments and
engagements that had been scheduled before I knew
about the surgery.

"Try to reschedule as soon as possible," I had said
to those who do my bookings. I figured I would be
back out on the speaking tour in no more than two
months.

I did put my will in order, however.

The one last thing I felt I needed to do was give
a party. I decided to have it at my house on Saturday night after the P.V.I. (Pig Valve Invitational). I
wanted to be with as many of my friends as I could
possibly be with in my own home, and I wanted
them to see me going into this thing head up, eyes
straight, unafraid. For the last party I decided I
might have to drink a fairly large amount of vodka.
It was a gathering of eagles. I had guests from every part of my life. A friend of mine, on his death-
bed, once said to me, "I just wish I could be in the
same room one more time, with everybody I loved
and everybody who loved me."

This would be close.

I cried only once. It was when the boys from Moreland, my hometown, walked in, and we put our arms around each other and I told them I loved them and they told me they loved me. And that was before very much vodka, too.

The party had been sort of a last-minute deal, and Mike, the only one of us who lived in another state, couldn't make it.

But Bobby and Dudley and Danny did. We had been together since the second grade.

We damned creeks together, learned to smoke and drink beer together, fell in love together, played ball together, and spent practically every day for eleven years together. Danny went to Vietnam, then went to work for Delta. Dudley was in the navy and told them if they would send him to Vietnam with a gun, he would straighten things out, but he didn't want to take any orders. Dudley was that way. They didn't send Dudley to Vietnam because they didn't want to escalate the war, so when he got out of the navy, he moved back to Moreland, and now he sells heavy equipment to foreigners and does quite well with it.

Bobby and I went to the University of Georgia together, where we both majored in journalism. He's got a normal job.

There was a period after school where we didn't see each other that often. I married Nancy from our class. Dudley married Camilla, Nancy's best friend in school. Danny married a girl we didn't know. Bobby married a girl he met at Georgia.

Nancy and I divorced. So did Dudley and Camil-

la. So did Danny and his first wife. Bobby is still
married to his college sweetheart.

I ran the streets of Atlanta awhile, then remarried and moved to Chicago. Dudley remarried, too,
and had a daughter. Danny raised two kids with
his first wife, divorced, and then remarried. Bobby
lived in another town in Georgia.

Oddly, it was Camilla, Dudley's first wife and
still Nancy's best friend (Nancy remarried soon after we divorced and lives—happily—with her husband and two sons in another state), who was
responsible for getting us back together, and keeping us that way.

I published my first book in 1979, and the publisher scheduled an autograph party in the county
seat of Coweta, where Moreland is located. That
would be Earline Scott's little bookstore in
Newnan, thirty miles south of Atlanta. It was the
night before Thanksgiving. The autographing ses-
sion was a rousing success. It lasted two hours
longer than scheduled, and Camilla had dropped by
toward the end and invited me to her apartment—
she had not remarried after Dudley—for a drink.

I went. Dudley, of all people, walked in. Then
Danny came with his wife. We told and retold every
old story, and the thing went all night and became
an annual event. For this book, I will do a signing
in Earline Scott's new bookstore on the square in
Newnan, and we'll all gather at Camilla's again.
Bobby has been coming now for years, as well.

We talk about how Dudley drove like a wild man
in high school and how amazing it was we survived

riding with him. And the time Danny got a new football for Christmas when we were twelve, but he never took the thing out of the box because he didn't want to get it dirty, and we all laughed and said, "Somewhere in a closet, he's still got that football."

When Bobby was twelve and thirteen and fourteen, he was a great hitter for the Moreland boys' baseball team, which dominated all our opponents. Then he went on to play Babe Ruth League and high school ball and never got another base hit.

"You were oh-for-adolescence," I like to kid him.

They get on me for telling the school bully they'd been making fun of him one day. They all tell me again what a fool I was for letting Nancy get away from me, too. They're right.

Dudley was the wild one in school. Danny, the quiet one. Bobby, the schemer. I guess I was the dreamer. But we were close back then, and we've done that bonding thing over and over again, so I had this plan that night at the party.

I had a song I wanted to sing to the boys from Moreland. This will take just a short explanation.

I mentioned in the very first chapter of this book I can sing a lick, and I mean just a lick. I was doing a lot of comedy shows around the South, and this guy had an idea that maybe I should put some music in my show, some original music.

Since he knew I knew nothing whatsoever about music, he also knew I needed some help. Through some connections in Nashville, he came up with the name Dick Feller.

Dick Feller, for the uninformed, has written some great country songs. He wrote the sound track for the movie *Smokey and the Bandit*, including Jerry Reed's hit "East Bound and Down." He wrote another Jerry Reed hit called, "Lord, Mr. Ford," and he wrote "Some Days Are Diamonds," which John Denver recorded.

Dick Feller and I sat down to write some country tunes together. They were all supposed to be funny. Some were. We do them in the shows. Sometimes the people laugh right out loud, and I *think* it's at the words, not my singing. But some of the songs came out downright sentimental.

Before Dick and I began to work together, Dick did something very strange—he sat down and read every book I'd ever written, and because of that, he knew more about my work than I did.

One day he said to me, "There's a story in one of your books about your old friends from home. You guys get together after a while, at Camilla's house, but when you leave, you say you didn't hug them and you didn't tell them you loved them because . . . 'You know how grown men are.'"

Dick Feller said he really liked that line, *You know how grown men are.*

And so a song came out of that one line, and I'm damn proud of that song, and what I wanted to do was sing it to Dudley and Danny and Bobby that night at the party.

No way I could have done it, though. I have trouble not crying when I do it with Dick onstage, a thousand miles from Moreland. But I want to offer the words here. Men do not have much left but each other anymore, if you will pardon the antipolitically correct jab, so this is for the boys of Moreland, if they read this far. If they don't, somebody show them to the page:

The song is entitled "Absent Friends":

> "Now and then, I run into
> Some boyhood friend of mine
> And we tell those old war stories
> And recall those ol' times
> And we point to our middles
> And we laugh about our hair
> And we say we should get together soon,
> But we never say when or where
>
> (Chorus)
> " 'Cause you know how grown men are
> Afraid to touch,
> We love each other from afar
> But the rhymes of the children
> Become the dreams of old men,
> And I have loved you dearly
> My absent friends
>
> (Bridge)
> "They say time moves like molasses
> When you are children
> But it rages like a river
> When you're grown
> But the love of the pals of my childhood
> Remains the truest love I've ever known

(repeat chorus)
"But you know how grown men are
Afraid to touch,
We love each other from afar
But the rhymes of the children
Become the dreams of old men
And I have loved you dearly
My absent friends.

(spoken)
    "And, so tonight, I lift a glass to Bobby,
Danny,
    Dudley and Mike ... and to all my absent
friends."

That's what I wanted to sing. That's what I wanted
to say. *The rhymes of the children become the
dreams of old men.* We aren't old men yet, I wanted
to say, but we're tracking.

"And if I should die before you do," maybe another line in the song should have gone—or I could
have said that night, "Know it was damn fine to
have scaled manhood beside you."

Yeah, I could have said that. But you know how
grown men are.

So it was a fine party. I don't remember it end-
ing.

I met Dedra Kyle Tiramani, former homecoming
queen from Cleveland, Tennessee, three-and-a-half

years ago in an Atlanta restaurant named Chops. I walked in with my date, who announced she had to go to the rest room before we were seated. I wasn't particularly fond of my date, but it was a barren period. I walked along the bar, and suddenly, I was standing behind all the hair on earth.

"I must see," I said to myself, "just what and who this is on the other side of that hair."

So I pulled an old trick.

I leaned to the right of the hair and said to the bartender, "double Stoli, tall glass, rocks, with orange juice neat."

"Good evening, Mr. Grizzard," said the bartender.

The hair turned to her right. She was lovely. Looked very Italian. Late twenties. My date likely was already flushing by now. I had to work fast.

I introduced myself and asked the hair her name.

"Dedatajazzzi," is what it sounded like she said.

"Deda," I said, "I'll be honest with you. My dinner date is in the rest room, and she will be coming out soon, so I don't have much time. I promise I don't make a habit of this sort of thing, but I would really like to call you later and take you out. Could I have your telephone number?"

I could get her name down later. This Italian beauty reminded me of a girl I met in Harry's Bar in Florence once. Harry's Bar and Grill in Florence, S.C., by the way.

She gave me her phone number. I was very pleasantly surprised. I had halfway expected the "Get lost, creep" routine.

I had the veal chop. My date had the crabs.

I called Hair for a date. It turned out she lived in
Auburn, Alabama, one hundred miles south of Atlanta. She lived with her year-old daughter, Jordan. She had recently divorced her husband in Fort
Lauderdale and had moved to Auburn, where her
mother and her stepfather lived.

I got the name straight—she was the former
Dedra Kyle, and that was Cherokee not Italian in
her face—and yes, she would like to have a date
with me.

(Later, she said she once dated a guy who read
my column every day and liked what I had to say,
and the reason she went out with me was because
she was curious.)

Our first date, we went to an outdoor Frank
Sinatra concert in Atlanta. We drank wine and ate
prosciutto.

I gave her an engagement ring in February 1993.

☞ ♥ ☜

Timothy Kevin Jarvis, former hippie, joined the
Midtown Racquet Club in Chicago in 1976. He was
a Chicago native and needed a place to play tennis
indoors during the cold Chicago months.

Tim had a degree in engineering and a degree
in social work. He was married to a Puerto Rican
wife. They counseled Puerto Rican families in Chicago, and Tim also led encounter groups and had
already learned to be sensitive.

I was in Chicago in 1976 as well, as sports editor
of the *Chicago Sun-Times*. I had joined the Midtown in December of the previous year. When Tim

joined, the pro had given him a list of names and telephone numbers of members at his tennis level.

Tim called me. We arranged a match. He won the first three games. I won the match, 6–3, 6–1. We played another set. I won that, 6–0.

Tim Jarvis and I would play tennis with and against each other nearly every day for the next decade. We also would become almost brotherly. And how different we were.

Tim not only had been a card-carrying hippie, he'd tripped on acid, marched against the war, voted for George McGovern, and thought Jane Fonda was a heroine.

I missed the drug scene entirely, voted for Nixon (both times), and still think Jane Fonda should be hanged as a traitor.

I was a Southerner and damn proud of it. Tim was a Yankee and didn't know any better.

First we had tennis. Then Tim found out I was the guy who fired a sportswriter he absolutely hated at the *Sun-Times*, and he gained some respect for me for that.

I found in him a male friend with whom I could be completely honest. I found in him a male friend who once cried with me.

I moved back to Atlanta in 1977. A few months later, Tim came to visit me, fell in love with the city, and wound up divorcing his wife and moving in with me. We were friends, we were brotherlike, we were a doubles tennis team. Not a very good doubles tennis team, but a doubles tennis team nonetheless.

(To be perfectly honest about out tennis situation, I beat Tim the first hundred times we played singles. After he moved to Atlanta, he took six months off from gainful employment and hung out at a place called the Bitsy Grant Tennis Center every day. Suddenly, I couldn't get a set off him anymore, and he and another guy were once the second-ranked thirty-five-and-over doubles team in the South.)

Tim and I both had to quit tennis because of injuries, his back, my arm. After that, we shared golf.

Tim made me a little more liberal. I made him a little more conservative. I can still tell him things I would never tell anybody else about myself.

Tim remarried and moved to California, where he is in business with his brother. One day, he will move back to Atlanta.

☞ ♥ ☜

Stephen Lee Enoch is my agent. He books my speeches and my little road shows. He talks to people on the phone, especially people I don't want to talk to.

Steve is from Richmond, Virginia. He went to the University of Miami. He is a blond, handsome man who has been married twice. He has two children.

I joined a golf club on Daufuskie Island, South Carolina, a boat ride from Hilton Head, several years ago. So did Steve. It's called the Melrose Club. That's where we met.

We played in the annual member-member tournament there one year. On the second day, Steve shot 68, and we won the tournament.

People asked, "Did you help?"

"Hell, yeah," I replied, "I said, 'Great shot, partner' all afternoon."

Steve is my agent, a golf partner, and he is a dear friend.

☞ ♥ ☜

Dedra Kyle Tiramani, her daughter, Jordan, four and a half, and Timothy Kevin Jarvis got into the car with me Sunday at eleven A.M., March 21, 1993, and the four of us drove to Emory Hospital. Had my mother been alive, and able, I'd have wanted her with me, too.

☞ ♥ ☜

There is a wonderful drug called Ativan. You take it, and you are no longer a part of this world. You still walk and talk, but you don't remember any of it, and it does one fine number on anxiety.

After I checked into my room at Emory and a nurse or two came in with this and that to say, one gave me some Ativan. I was lying in the bed. Tim was sitting in a chair to the right of the bed. Dedra was standing at the foot of the bed. Jordan, who is blond with gorgeous green eyes, was everywhere.

That's it. That's the last thing I remember. It couldn't have been any later than early Sunday afternoon, and it would still be the next morning before I went to surgery, but it would still be basically the last piece of reality I would experience for over two weeks. Gone for two weeks. Checked out. East with the geese.

So what I offer here for what transpired during that period is all from what I have been told later by others. There are the dreams about which I can report firsthand, but all that happened outside my brain—and it was quite a lot—must come from conversations I had later with family and friends and nurses and doctors and even from reading newspaper accounts.

That is frightening within itself. I am not a person who likes to give up control. It's one of the reasons I've always had trouble with flying. When I'm up there, I'm at somebody else's mercy.

And for two weeks at Emory, somebody could have made the decision to have my head removed and replaced with an amazing Ronco Veg-o-matic, and I could have done not one thing about it.

(As a matter of fact, it is rumored somebody did suggest that but was told plastic surgery was done on another floor.)

Nobody could have predicted what was about to happen to me. My cardiologist knew this was to be my third surgery, and certainly there were more risks than, say, my first. And my surgeon, going in for the third time, knew even better. He had repaired my infected heart seven years earlier.

But he had talked about those risks.

"It's my gut feeling you'll do fine," Dr. Martin had said.

Dr. Jones, recall, had talked about how there might be a problem with excessive bleeding because of excessive scar tissue in the area where he would be working.

They had those *experimental drugs*.

No test could have foreseen the problems. You can listen to a heart and see images of it and run tubes into it, but no sort of test or procedure can be 100 percent, dead-solid, balls-on accurate.

But I already mentioned previous warnings. *We are warned,* Mama said.

There was one more. This is strange, I admit it. But so is thinking of the possibility of having your head removed while somebody replaces it with an amazing Ronco Veg-o-matic. I never said I was normal:

I was driving along one day, maybe ten years ago. I happened to look down at the digital clock in my car. It was something like 3:03. I don't know why I suddenly thought of this, but it occurred to me, has there ever been a time in history when the year, month, day, hour, minute, and second were all the same number?

I continued driving and continued to give that some serious thought. (I once asked myself: *When women tennis players put that extra ball up their skirts while serving, where does it go?* I never figured out an answer to that question but just know I am prone to pondering such things.)

So I started thinking about numbers. Let's take four and deal simply with B.C. In 4 B.C., on April 4, at four minutes after four A.M. and P.M., if all that could have showed on a digital clock, it still wouldn't have showed all 4s. It would have been the year 4, the month and day 4/4, but the time would have 4:04. So, there's a zero in there, and there goes 4.

I thought of a few other numbers before finally figuring out the number had to be 1.

In the year 1111, on November 11, it was 11 seconds after 11 minutes after 11 hours on the 11th day of the 11th month.

This wasn't any great discovery, but I prided myself on being probably the first person even to think of that question, much less the first person to take, say, fifteen minutes to figure out an answer to it.

I didn't tell anybody about any of this at the time because I knew they would think I was weird.

But then something strange started happening to me. I actually began being haunted by the numbers "1111." It seemed that every time I looked at a digital clock, it said 11:11.

Food products, I noticed, would have November 11 as their expiration date. Radio announcers were always saying in my ear, "It's eleven past eleven here in . . ."

At first I thought this was simply coincidence and some sort of odd power of suggestion.

But it dragged on for years. There is a digital clock on the oven in my kitchen. It stopped working.

At 11:11.

I was sitting on a beach in Hilton Head. I struck up a conversation with a couple under the next umbrella. They had twin girls.

"How old are your twins?" I asked.

"They're both eleven," I was told.

I would by things at convenience stores. The bill would come to $11.11. (If a certain convenience store had changed its name to 11-Eleven, I might have jumped off a bridge.)

I'd really never been superstitious in my life until this thing. I stopped flying on November 11. I stopped looking at clocks and my watch unless I knew it was at least two hours before or after eleven.

I'm not certain exactly when I made the connection with this bit of madness and my surgery, but it did eventually come.

—March 22, 1993, was exactly eleven years to the day since my first heart surgery.

—Twenty-two is eleven and eleven added together.

"Nah," I kept telling myself. "This is silly."

But I couldn't get it out of my mind. I even broke down and mentioned it to friends. They looked at me as if I were crazy.

Well, not all of them. I was telling my friend Dick McDonald about it all—after four double Grizzards in a bar a few weeks before entering the hospital—and he said, "Don't worry about it. My birthday is on the eleventh, my name is McDonald, and that's your middle name."

(My paternal grandmother was a McDonald.)

Mike Matthews is another friend of mine. He named his son Michael Lewis in my honor. I told him about the eleven thing.

"Michael Lewis was born on the eleventh," he pointed out. "No problem."

I made certain not to check into Emory on Sunday until after noon. If my room number had an eleven in it anywhere, they would still be trying to find me.

Dedra had a small cot in my hospital room for Sunday night. Steve went home, and Tim went back to my house. If I dreamed, I don't remember it. I would find out later they came to take me to the operating room at six the next morning.

I was awake before that, however. Dedra says I was yakking away with a nurse at 4:30, which awakened her. Tim and Steve came at five.

"The first thing you wanted," Steve said, "was to go in the bathroom and have a smoke. So, we went in there and fired up a couple."

"I had a cigarette in the hospital room?" I asked.

"We both had a Marlboro Medium," Steve said.

Even I can't imagine sneaking a cigarette in the bathroom of a hospital room an hour before going down for heart surgery. It had to be the medication.

"There was a lot that went on in the bathroom," said Dedra later.

That frightened me even more than the deal about the cigarette.

"You don't mean I asked you . . . ?"

"You'd rather have had the cigarette," said Dedra. "You wanted to talk to me about your funeral."

My funeral?

The only semiofficial decision I'd ever made

about a thing like that was once my stepfather, soon after my mother died in 1990, asked me if anything happened to me, did I want to be buried in the family plot in Moreland?

I had said, "Yeah, bury me next to Mama."

I had said that because I couldn't think of anything else to say at the time. How I wanted to be disposed of after death had never really been a major concern of mine. I always figured, what did it matter to me, I'd be dead.

Frankly, however, I didn't really like any of the obvious choices. I'd always gotten spooked when they lowered caskets into the ground. I've always been a little claustrophobic, and I worried about worms eating me. I know the casket goes into a steel vault these days. (I remember picking out my mother's casket and the funeral director telling us the vault was guaranteed for fifty years and thinking, Yeah? and how can you verify that?), but I still worried about worms.

And if dust is supposed to go back to dust, how would my dust get out of the vault and the casket to blend back in with the red clay earth of Georgia?

Then there was cremation, but the idea of getting burned, even if I was dead, was not too appealing, either.

I wondered if there was anything beyond that. Once I thought, Maybe they could just put me under a tree and guard me from the worms and buzzards until I rotted away and blended in with the ground. But I found out that was against the law and would be terribly ghoulish and uncomfortable for even good friends and close family.

Then I thought about what my stepbrother Ludlow Porch once said about Roy Rogers:

"When Bullet [Roy's dog] died, he had him stuffed and put into his museum. When Trigger [Roy's horse] died, he did the same thing. I just hope Dale [Roy's wife] outlives him."

But I thought being stuffed wouldn't be so bad. They could stuff me and put me somewhere. There is actually a museum of sorts in my hometown of Moreland now. They turned the old knitting mill into a museum featuring artifacts of the way people lived and farmed a hundred years ago. They could put me in that museum in some glass. I visited the Vatican once. There are five-hundred-year-old popes under the glass in there.

I had not put any thought into my funeral plans before my third operation, however; I suppose I just subconsciously ignored it all. But Dedra said I awakened that Monday morning with it very much on my mind.

"You asked me to come into the bathroom with you and bring a pen and paper," she said. "Once we got inside, you said, 'Write all this down. This is what I want, in case I die.'"

She kept the paper. She showed it to me after I'd returned home from the hospital.

I had decided I wanted to be cremated after all. I had wanted my ashes spread over Sanford Stadium, on the campus of the University of Georgia. I had told Dedra that if she couldn't get permission, to sneak in at night and do it. I'm certain the Georgia Athletic Department gets a lot of requests like that, and if they allowed everybody who wanted his or her ashes strewn over the field, it eventually would do harm to the lovely turf.

I said I wanted to have a memorial service of sorts, held outdoors on the first tee at the Ansley Golf Club in Atlanta, where I am a member. It is a quarter-mile from my house. I asked Dedra to find a sweet girl with a pretty voice to sing one song, "Precious Memories," which was sung at my mother's funeral, and to give anybody who wanted to the opportunity to say a few words.

"You'd better keep it under some control, though," I pointed out, "because if the crowd gets bored with the eulogy, a gin game will break out." They're mad to play gin at Ansley.

I asked her to contact the Reverend Gilbert Steadham, who had been the Methodist minister when I was a boy in Moreland, to come and offer a prayer. Preacher Steadham, as country folks call their ministers, had been around when my father was battling the bottle as well as whatever it is that makes a man go crazy after two wars, and had tried his best to help him. The preacher was one of the few who never gave up on him.

"Tell him," I said, "to assure everybody I went to heaven. 'Cause there will be some doubts."

Then Dedra said I told her to buy a headstone and put it in the plot in the Moreland Methodist Cemetery and to place it next to my mother's.

"Anything special you want on the stone?" she said she asked me.

"Put my name and when I was born and died," I answered, "and then put, 'He once shot par.' "

"You really want me to put that on your gravestone?"

"I do," I said. "Do you know how many people can actually say they've shot par? Not many."

Then, Dedra said, I launched into a full explanation of the time I did, in fact, shoot par 71 at the Greensboro (N.C.) Country Club.

"Anything else?" she wanted to know.

"After the memorial service," I had gone, "throw a party. Rent a big room in a hotel somewhere, and I'll leave enough money to have a band like the Swinging Medallions to play fifties music. And get some barbecue for everybody and lots of booze. And set up some tables, because there will be some guys from Ansley who will get bored with the music and want to play gin."

Dedra had all that on the paper she gave me later. I told her to put it in a safe place.

Steve said some people came into the room with a rolling bed a minute or so before six.

"We had gone back into the bathroom for one last cigarette, by the way," he also mentioned.

"Strangest thing, though," he went on. "Just before they wheeled you out, a young nurse walked over to you and asked you the damndest question. She asked, 'Mr. Grizzard, are you allergic to anything?' I thought, What a helluva time to be asking that."

Steve has never had much experience with the medical profession, due to the fact he's healthy, despite the Marlboro Mediums, and doesn't understand that question. They ask you that question in doctor's offices and hospitals more than "Who is going to be responsible for your bill?"

The medical profession is keen on covering its ass these days, which it must be, in lieu of the fact malpractice lawyers own a lot of yachts. Before they stick something in your body or make you take a pill, they want to make sure you aren't going to break out in some sort of horrid rash, lose the ability to breathe, or go goobers and run outside in the path of an oncoming bus.

So they always ask you, "Are you allergic to anything?"

I always say, "I don't think so," because I'm not really sure. Nothing they've ever given me before has caused me to do any of the aforementioned.

I've had enough antibiotics in my life to know I'm not allergic to those, and isotopes don't turn my hair multicolored or make me want to show up at sporting events with religious posters.

I admitted to Steve later, however, I also thought that was a rather silly time to be asking me what I might be allergic to. Wouldn't that be the sort of thing that should be discovered long before only a scant few minutes prior to heart surgery?

"From the way you answered the question," Steve said, "I sort of got the idea you felt that way, too."

I made the mistake of asking Steve how I had answered the question.

"Well," he began, "they were rolling you out of the room, and you asked them to stop right in front of the nurse, and you said, 'As a matter of fact, my good woman, there is something I am allergic to. It's snake poison. It causes me to swell.

" 'Recently,' you went on, 'I was out in the woods and was bitten by the dreaded copperhead water rattler—the meanest snake on earth. If you check into a Holiday Inn to get away from one, they will take the room next to your room and bite you when you are checking out the next morning—on the very end of my little thing.' "

"I said, 'little thing'?" I asked Steve incredulously.

"That's how you described it, yes," he answered.

"Good."

"Anyway, you said, 'That thing swole [Southern for 'swelled'] up so big you just couldn't believe it. I mean, it was ten times bigger than its normal size.

" 'Knowing I had very little time to live, I rushed out of the woods, got into my car, and drove to a nearby general store, run by two old maids. I walked into the store, in great pain, showed one of the old maids my problem, and asked, "What can you give me for this?"

" 'She said, "Let me check with my sister." In a few moments, she came back and said, "Would you take the store, a '47 Packard, and thirty-eight acres of land?" '

There is something else I don't remember about

Sunday at Emory. Something else I'm *happy* I don't remember. That was the shave.

They didn't tell me about the shave before my first heart surgery. Here is the deal on that: Surgeons don't want a lot of hair around where they have to work. Plus, a lot of hair in the operating room could cause infections.

So what they do to valve-replacement patients, at least, is shave them from their necks to their knees. The only parts they don't shave in that area are the arms and the hands. Underarms, yes, but not the other parts of the arms. Why? I don't know. I'm neither a doctor nor a barber.

I remember the first two shaves. They were done by men. Getting shaved by another man on the neck is normal. I've had barbers shave me there. The chest is a little hairier, if you will. And the underarms, even more testy. Men should never be without their underarm hair, I remember thinking, just because it is, in this country, at least, a sure sign of manliness. Like understanding the infield-fly rule.

I had to lose my hairy thighs, too. Hairy thighs are macho, and Harry Thigh, a third baseman, was up for a brief cup of coffee with the '59 Sox, I remembered, before being sent back down to Triple A.

"I'm going to get the family jewels now," I recall the man saying who shaved me before my first surgery.

We are talking big-league uncomfortable here,

because in order to get to those to shave them, the
shaver must lift another man's Johnson.

"Do hurry," I said to the shaver.

This time, however, it was different. Dedra knew
how much I dreaded that shave, so she volunteered
to do it, and they let her.

Only Dedra got carried away and shaved everything south of my neck, including my arms and
hands and even south of my knees.

"It was fun," she said. "I'd never done anything
like that."

That's why chicken pluckers do what they do, I
suppose.

☞ ♥ ☜

I'm not certain at what point the angels gathered
and began hovering around me. There had to be a
few at least. I believe in angels. My grandmother
did, too.

When I was growing up, my grandmother and I
had walked a quarter-mile to Cureton and Cole's
store in Moreland late one afternoon. She needed
snuff, as I recall. It was my grandmother's only
vice, snuff. She dipped Bruton's. Mama Willie
would sit in her chair in her tiny living room, read
the Bible, and enjoy whatever the enjoyment is in
snuff, moving her head from the blessed word only
to expunge into her tin spit cup, which she dutifully washed out after each dipping.

As we walked back down the dirt road that led to
our house, we had to pass the Moreland Baptist
Church. An old man, dressed in rags, was lying

near the entrance to the church. My grandmother was a member there. My mother and I went to Moreland Methodist a quarter-mile away. My mother had moved to the other side after marrying my father, who came from a long line of Methodists.

My grandfather, despite being a deeply religious man, wouldn't go to either of the Moreland churches. After attending the Baptist once he noticed the minister was using notes. He didn't believe in ministers using notes. He believed the message was supposed to be piped in directly from above.

He also believed in the washing of feet. That's what they had done at the Baptist church where he had grown up. On Sundays, they washed each other's feet in church to show their humbleness and love of their fellow man. (You didn't have to say "person" in those days, so I won't.) Jesus, recall, had done that, too.

I was eight or nine. When I saw the old man, I said to my grandmother, "Think we ought to call the law?"

I had thought, That old man shouldn't be there at Mama Willie's church. He's probably going to steal something.

I had seen enough television by that time to be suspicious of strangers. A stranger in town will steal a horse or rob a bank every time.

"That man may be hungry," said Mama Willie.

We walked over to the man. Mama Willie asked him if he was hungry, and he said he was. He said he hadn't eaten in days, as a matter of fact, and that he had come to the church hoping to find somebody who would feed him. He had found some-one.

When my grandmother, my grandfather, my mother, and myself sat down to a pork chop and fresh vegetables table that night, the old man was with us. I opened my own eyes to make certain his were closed when my grandfather said the blessing. They were.

After dinner, Mama Willie made the man a bed in the back of our wooden garage. She fed him again the next morning and also gave him one of my grandfather's shirts to replace the tattered one he was wearing.

The man thanked Mama Willie for half an hour and then disappeared up the dirt road. We never saw him again.

Mama Willie said, after he had gone, "You never know when God will send an angel down from heaven in that shape just to see if anybody will help."

I suppose that's one of the reasons I've always been such a soft touch for beggars on the streets. There is no telling how much Gallo Thunderbird wine I have bought for visiting angels over the years.

Winos usually have great stories. I've heard, "I've just driven in from Little Rock with my family, and I need money for the baby's formula."

I know that what he needs is his own formula, but I come through with a little change anyway.

I'm a sucker for WILL WORK FOR FOOD, too. The

only work I usually have for anybody is to write the next column for me, so I wind up just handing over some money.

A few months before all this befell me, I was home on a Sunday afternoon. The doorbell rang, and there stood a man with two small boys. His story was that he had come to Atlanta from Houston with his sons for a job, but that the job had fallen through. He said he was trying to get back to Houston and needed exactly $47.50 for the rest of the cost of bus tickets for the three.

The two boys were looking up at me with hungry eyes. My grandmother was looking down on me. So what was I supposed to do?

In these more cynical times, my first thought was, It's the old I-need-$47.50-for-bus-tickets-back-to-Houston trick. They work ten neighborhoods a weekend.

But before I knew it, my hand was reaching into my pocket, and out came a $100 bill. What was I going to do—ask the man for change?

"A HUNDRED DOLLARS!" the man said to his two boys.

"We can go home! We can go home!"

So maybe I got stiffed. But when they were getting up a group of angels to go down to Emory to look over me that March morning, a spokesangel had to say, "Get five more. Don't forget he forked over the C-note to the guy and the two kids."

Had the doctors known what they were going to face when they sliced me open that morning, they might not even have attempted the operation.

"We can't mess around with anything like this," they would have said. "He would die on the operating table."

They would have sent me home to die, at my own convenience.

But down I went toward Emory's operating room 4. Dedra, armed with the funeral plans, Steve, puffing nervously on the Marlboro Mediums, and Tim went to the waiting room. Friends and family gathered.

One angel said to another, "This isn't going to be easy."

The other replied, "Just do what you can. Mama Willie said he was a good boy and never opened his eyes during the blessing."

✷✷✷ 6 ✷✷✷

I NOW HAVE IN MY POSSESSION A CHRONOLOGY OF WHAT
happened to me over the next thirty-six days.

It begins like this:

3/21: Admitted.

3/22: In O.R. (operating room) 4. Sedation begins
at 6:39 A.M.

9:00 A.M.: Cooled to 24 Celsius.

10:44: Cardiopulmonary bypass started. Root replaced with St. Jude #27 and Dacron conduit—
valve sealed with 2-0 Tevdek sutures on Teflon felt
pledgets—4-0. Prolene-sutured left main coronary
artery to conduit.

12:30: Rewarm begins.

12:52: Aorta cross-clamp removed. Retrocardiac
bleeding.

12:55: Rewarm and aorta cross-clamped. No left ventricular function (electrical or mechanical activity)—saphenous veins harvested from legs and left anterior descending and obtuse marginal bypassed.

15:31: Rewarmed to 37 degrees. LV function good by intrap TEE, but right ventricle poor.

16:00: Intraortic balloon pump placed in left femoral artery, RCA bypassed, epicardial pacer wires placed. Chest tubes in both pleural cavities and mediastinum.

19:00: Arrhythmia with biventricular failure.

20:40: RVAD/LVAD placed as lifesaving maneuver.

23:57: To intensive-care unit. RVAD/LVAD, intubated. Epinephrine, amrinone, Vanco, and Gent. Heavily sedated. Transplant evaluation. Placed on transplant list.

05:57: O.R. 4. Reexplored for bleeding and clots. Rubber dam removed and massive clots removed from mediastinum fibrin glue, surgical, lap pads for hemostasis. Chest closed.

17:30: To ICU.

Allow me to translate all that for you: All hell broke loose.

"We waited and we waited and we waited," Dedra told me much later. "We were in that waiting room for hours and hours, and we just never did hear anything.

"I began to get mad. I said, 'You'd think they would at least let us know how it's going.' I kept asking everybody else, because we didn't hear anything, if they thought everything was okay. They kept assuring me it was, but I started to get this feeling.

"Something had to be wrong. Dr. Martin wouldn't just let us sit up here without a word if he knew he could come up and tell us we could relax. The more I thought about it, the more I convinced myself something was dreadfully wrong.

"At two that afternoon, I was crazy. I finally said, 'I can't stand this.' I went to a phone and called Dr. Martin's office and demanded to talk to him. They put me on hold. Finally, he came to the phone and put it pretty bluntly. He said, 'It doesn't look good.' "

The doctors had been too busy trying to save my life to call anybody.

I sat down with Dr. Martin and one of his assistants two months after I left the hospital, and I wanted to know exactly what transpired and exactly what was done. They gave me the chronology I referred to earlier; they also tried to explain each step verbally to me, so I could understand and so that I would be able to put it all forth here for the reader.

To be honest about it, I've worried for weeks if I'm really going to be able to pull this off. Things get really technical here, and I'm not very technical. I'm pretty good with "on" and "off" buttons, but after that, I'm usually lost.

So what I've decided to do, for all our sakes, is simply tell you what I understand happened, and try to keep the medicalese to a minimum. If I don't, we'll get up to our ears in ooplescoptomies and rabbledingdongamees and filladips and QVDs and ORPDs and rancamiacine and limbaughsectomies (putting good sense into the head of a liberal) and confusion will run rampant across these pages, as my editor often says of my prose.

There will be medical people who will read this, of course, and they will respond by saying, "Do what?"

But this isn't for them. This is for those of us who have to lie down in a hospital, which is something else I have learned during all my heart and health problems: When it comes to heart and health problems, try never to be the one lying down. It's the people standing up who aren't sick.

Here we go:

At 21 minutes until 7 A.M., March 22, 1993, they started sticking tubes in me. They call them "lines." Then they started shooting various medicines through these lines.

This takes quite a while. They stick lines in your neck and arms and legs, and in go the various medical juices.

There is also some waiting that occurs. Have you ever been involved with anything pertaining to medicine that didn't involve waiting? The surgeon has to get ready. The assistants, the nurses, and anesthesiologist, all have to get ready. I presume they didn't have to finish a hot gin game, but there are things that have to be done in preparation.

So you lie there on your table oblivious to it all. I don't know how anybody looks at a time like this, but I did run into a nurse once who helped put in my lines for a previous operation. She said to me, "You look a lot better than you did the last time I saw you outside that operating room." She said that to me at one in the morning in a bar, which indicates one probably doesn't look one's best at the moment we are discussing.

So, I'm good and sedated. Then, at nine in the morning, the cooling process began. The reason a body is cooled is to get the heart to stop beating. You can't operate on a heart while it's beating, no matter how steady the hands.

At that point, they had to get to my heart. The anesthesiologist does his thing, and then I was opened. I like that term, "opened." It's better than "sliced" or "dug into," "gutted," or just plain "cut," which is what happens to people in Southern beer joints who mess with somebody else's wife or insult another's bird dog.

I don't think the surgeon opens. I think somebody else, a minion, does that. I was told before my first surgery that the reason there is not a lot of postoperative pain, in relation to other sorts of surgeries, is no tissue is cut when the chest is opened. Feel your chest. There is just a small layer of skin between the outside of you and your sternum.

So now we're somewhere around ten in the morning, and I've been opened and there is my sternum. You've got to get through that piece of bone, of course, before reaching the heart. The first time, they sliced through my sternum. I have never seen the instrument used to do this, but I've always imagined it to look like something akin to a small saw, something one might find in a Black & Decker catalog.

Right down the middle of the sternum goes the saw, bone fragments flying hither, thither, and yon . . . and there's the heart.

In my case, this being my third surgery, what they had to do to get to my heart was unwire me. Once the sternum is sawed open, it is wired back together following surgery. When one looks at one's X rays after this, it appears as if one may have swallowed a chain-link fence.

The wires came out, my sternum was loose, and, from what I have been told, it was then stretched hither, thither, etc., and there was the heart, looking up from its gooey cavity from where it performs its miraculous life-giving support of the rest of the body.

Meanwhile, the rest of me was completely covered, there wasn't a germ in miles, every part of my person was being monitored very closely, and I had a breathing tube down my throat. My brain was in Nova Scotia, so I didn't know anything, which was a wondrous blessing.

They cooled my heart until it stopped beating. At fifteen minutes until eleven, I went on heart-lung bypass. This is the cardiopulmonary machine that pumps the blood through the rest of the body for the heart while it is stilled for the surgery. Without that machine, heart surgery wouldn't be possible, and there would be a lot more graves than there are currently.

Dr. Ellis Jones began the operation. He replaced the old porcine valve with the St. Jude mechanical. He also had to do a lot of patchwork with Dacron and probably rayon, polyester, and who knows how much Reynolds aluminum wrap, and he had to solder this and grout this.

I kept wondering what a recording of all this would have sounded like:

"Clamp, Nurse."

"Clamp, Doctor."

"Dacron conduit."

"Dacron conduit."

"Suction."

"Suction."

"Rubber band."

"Rubber band."

"And a thumbtack if you can find one."

"Will a paper clip and a safety pin do?"

"More suction."

"Suction, Doctor."

"Two Tevdeck sutures on Teflon felt pledgets."

"Say again?"

"Another paper clip."

"Four-oh Prolene suture."

"Four-oh Prolene suture."

"SOS pad."

"SOS pad."

"Doohickey."

"Doohickey, Doctor."

"And a whatchamacallit."

"One whatchamacallit."

The surgeon was able to replace the valve, but he

found an awful mess in my heart. There was even more scar tissue, perilous leftovers from the tooth infection and the second surgery, than had been expected. The bleeding was worse than expected, too.

And my previous valve. Later, here's what frightened me more than anything else: The surgeon told me the 1985 valve was barely still attached. It was down to one or two sutures, and as he put it, "It's amazing it didn't just blow out months earlier."

I asked another question I wished I hadn't asked.

"What if that had happened?"

The answer was, "You probably wouldn't have made it alive to the nearest emergency room."

I walked around, for quite a while, on the brink of demise. I shot my par round in '91. Lord, what if the valve had gone as I stood over that last little putt on eighteen? I'd have gone ahead and putted out, I'm certain, making it even less likely I'd ever have made it to the nearest emergency room.

It's now 12:30 P.M. in O.R. 4. Dr. Jones has finished. He has battled all that was against him, and he has attached the new valve in my aorta. I'm still alive.

Rewarm begins.

Twenty-two minutes later, there's some more bleeding. It's getting to be a mess in my heart again. Another clamp is placed on my aorta in order to stop the blood. That doesn't do the job.

I'm still on the bypass. My heart is stopped. My chest is still open. I'm having blood transfusions by the washtubful. The bleeding is so bad, because of scar tissue and various other problems, I'm getting those experimental drugs I had heard about earlier.

"Things were that bad," a doctor said. "We were getting desperate to stop that bleeding."

The bleeding finally was under control, so, around one, I was taken off the heart-lung bypass. The idea at that point was for my heart to start beating again.

It wouldn't.

In the chronology, that's where it says, "no left ventricular function."

"We really had a problem now," Dr. Martin said. "We weren't certain why the heart wouldn't start again."

It was decided, quickly, that loose material around the aorta—material that came off when the old valve was taken out and the new one was attached—might have gone down into my coronary arteries, blocking the blood supply to my heart.

So Dr. Jones jumped back in and did the classic coronary-bypass surgery. He took the saphenous veins (the really big suckers on the inside of your legs) out of my legs, cut off a chunk of each, and replaced what could have been clogged portions of my coronary arteries. They do this to people with cholesterol problems. They've already done valve replacement on me, and a few minutes later they're ripping out the veins from my legs for bypass. This isn't good.

"That didn't work, either," said Dr. Martin, "and now your right ventricle wasn't functioning."

Well, somebody do something else.

Somebody did. We're all the way to six in the evening by now (friends and family have been notified that "it doesn't look good") and they install a balloonlike pump into the femoral artery in my groin to see if that would get my heart beating again.

It wouldn't.

Next a pacemaker was installed to the left of my stomach. Nothing.

Seven, eight o'clock at night.

I asked the doctor, "How many tubes do you think I had in my body by this point?"

He went over the list.

"Well, there was the Swan-Ganz catheter, one down your throat, a balloon pump, four chest-drainage tubes . . . I'd say fifteen at least."

At nine o'clock, I was a dead man.

"You should have died, no question," Dr. Martin said later. "We couldn't get your heart to work no matter what we tried, and we had to take you off the bypass sooner or later. You just can't live on one of those things indefinitely."

At 10:40 P.M., the last resort was tried. On the chronology, it was: "RVAD/LVAD placed as a life-saving maneuver."

An RVAD/LVAD is a Bi-Ventricular Assist Device. I was told they are "roller pumps," and they circulate the blood around the body, not in a pumping style, but just as a steady flow.

A patient cannot live on these machines for any long period of time, either, but they get the patient off the bypass machine, which is worse.

"We were just trying to buy a little time at this point," I was told.

At three minutes to midnight, I finally was taken to the intensive-care unit. I had been in the operating room for over seventeen hours. And all those doctors and nurses had been in there with me.

Dedra said, "We were all just too stunned to be tired."

Tim said, "I was just really trying to deal with what life would be without you."

Steve said, "It was fourth and long."

Normally, the patient is returned from the operating room with his chest stitched and closed. Not me. Nobody knew what lay ahead, so, as it was explained to me, a "rubber dam" was stretched across my chest so if surgeons had to go back in, all that would have to be done would be to remove that dam.

I remained out of it. "Heavily sedated" it says on the chronology.

At one in the morning, they started talking transplant. Nobody could think of a viable alternative.

I was placed on something called the National Transplant List. At every moment of every night and day, there are people all over the country in hospitals waiting for heart (as well as other organs, of course) transplants. As donors become available, they are sent to these patients in some sort of order that obviously has to do with a great many considerations, how long the patient can do without one being primary, I would imagine.

Nobody was certain I would make it through the night.

At three minutes to six the next morning, I was back in operating room 4. I was bleeding to death again.

The rubber dam was removed, and the bleeding was stopped again. At two minutes until eight, I'm back in ICU.

At 12:45 P.M., I'm rushed to O.R. 4 again, bleeding to death for a third time. Tough way to start the day.

For nearly seven more hours, I remained in O.R. 4. There were more transfusions and more of the experimental drugs to try to stop the bleeding. I had massive blood clots in my chest as well.

The bleeding stopped. Nobody knows exactly why.

Naturally, many reinforcements had been called in by this time, but those who started out with me—doctors and nurses, et al.—were still there. Sleepless, but still there.

It is seven-thirty in the evening, Tuesday, March 23, when they finally close my chest and send me back to ICU again. For all but six hours in a span of thirty-six, I have been in an operating room with my chest opened.

I am living because the roller pumps, not my heart, are supplying my blood to my body. I have technicians who must watch them around the clock to make certain they work perfectly. One small glitch and I could die.

And I cannot live indefinitely on these, either.

They are used only as a last resort, only as *lifesaving maneuvers*.

Friends told me later that doctors they knew who had heard news reports of my predicament had all said it was just a matter of time before I died.

Me, I'm so cut to pieces and have so much hardware in me, I'm given a drug to paralyze me completely through the night so I won't move and cause God knows what to happen.

"We had to use every drug in the state of Georgia," Dr. Martin said.

I didn't have to have another operation on Wednesday—that's the good news. The bad is that my kidneys decided if my heart wasn't going to beat, they might as well as quit, too. This is known as "renal-function deterioration." When you have that, they take you off the transplant list, since, with your kidneys giving it up, you probably wouldn't make it through a transplant operation, and the donor heart would be wasted.

On top of that, I developed a fever.

"Infections," said Dr. Martin.

Oh, shit, as they say in medical school.

The last thing it says on the Wednesday chronology is, "Sedation and vecuromium weaned without waking—concern about CNS [central nervous system] increased."

Holy shit, as they say just about everywhere. They're concerned about brain damage.

They began taking me off some of the drugs, but I wouldn't awaken. That could mean that because of all that had taken place in good ol' O.R. 4, and because of all the bleeding and clots and the roller pumps that were keeping me alive, I could have that old bugaboo, brain damage.

Tim said later, "One of the things that always amazed me was how you didn't even grow up in Chicago but could still remember the starting lineup of the '59 White Sox, not to mention Harry Thigh, and I grew up in Chicago and certainly couldn't. That's the first thing I thought about when they mentioned brain damage: 'He won't be able to remember Jim Landis played centerfield for the '59 Sox.' "

Turk Lown was a relief pitcher, by the way, just to further my legendary expertise in that regard.

Let us review exactly where I am at this point.

I ain't got a chance. My heart won't work. I won't wake up. My kidneys are trying to quit. I've got a fever and probably an infection. And I could have brain damage. And it's still two more days to the weekend.

Meanwhile, in the waiting room. . . .

☞ ♥ ☜

My Aunt Jessie is the next-to-oldest of my late mother's brothers and sisters. She and my Aunt Una, the youngest, are the only survivors of five children. I have no idea how old Jessie or Una are, and I'm not going to ask either of them. But Una must be in her early seventies, I would guess, and Jessie in her early eighties.

Both these women are very special to me. Una loved my daddy. Una's first husband left the apart-

ment one day to go on an errand right after World
War II and never returned. I mean, the man disappeared.
Forever. There were many conjectures as to
what happened to him, but, as my daddy used to
say to Una, "Miss Word [her maiden name], he had
to be a man of low intelligence to leave someone as
lovely as you, or he fell into a deep, deep hole."

Una moved to Arlington, Virginia, to live with
my dad and mother and me in the early fifties, just
before Korea. During that period, my mother was
still recovering from the illness that had beset her
in Arkansas, and I thought Una, who took care of
me, was my second mother.

During this time, she met a soldier in my father's
outfit, John Coutee of Louisiana, and they would
marry.

Una thought, and still does, my father had the
best sense of humor she's ever known.

"He could always make me laugh no matter how
blue I was," she has said so often. We are close,
Una and I.

My Aunt Jessie married young, and she and her
husband, Grover, moved to Moreland from the old
homeplace in Carroll County, to be near my grandparents.
They both worked for years in the Moreland
knitting mill.

After Mother and Daddy divorced, Mother and I
also moved to Moreland and lived with my grandparents
in the house next to Grover and Jessie.

Aunt Jessie bought one of the first TVs in
Moreland, so I spent a lot of time at her house. She

also led the world in country cooking, and I took many a meal with her.

Una and John had remained in Arlington, across the Potomac from Washington, while I was growing up in Moreland. But I saw Jessie every day, and, I learned early, she was not one to be trifled with.

Jessie didn't allow sass. She didn't allow slumping at the table. She didn't allow tracking dirt into her house, and she didn't allow anybody trespassing through her flowers after a baseball. Jessie and her flowers.

People came from as far away as LaGrange, Hogansville, Corinth, and Rocky Mount just to look at Jessie's flowers. I don't know what sort of flowers Jessie grew, but they were everywhere, and they were quite colorful, indeed, and I can remember a woman getting out of her car once and walking up to Jessie, working in her yard at the time, and saying, "I come here every year just to look at your flowers. I really believe this is what heaven is going to look like."

One of my favorite pastimes as a small boy was standing in my grandmother's yard, throwing up a baseball and hitting it into the air. Not often, but occasionally, I would catch one flush so that it would carry into Aunt Jessie's yard and roll into one of her precious flower beds.

It's been nearly forty years, but I can still hear her:

"Young man! You get out of those flowers, or I'm going to wear you out!"

She never did wear me out, but I think she would

have if she ever thought I'd harmed even one petal
of one flower on purpose. I never did that, of
course. I simply would try to explain, "I'm sorry,
Aunt Jessie. I just hit it too far."

After John retired from the army, he and Una
moved to Moreland. Uncle Grover died. Aunt Jessie
still lives in her same house.

Una remains shy and even demure. She and
John came back and forth every day to Emory from
Moreland, as did Jessie, who is anything but shy. If
it comes to Jessie's mind, she says it. No matter
what.

As my closest blood relatives, my aunts were
talked to by doctors about the possibility of the
transplant. There were considerations as to how I
might feel if I awakened days later with somebody
else's heart.

Una was said to hedge a little. Jessie said to go
with it if they had to.

Dedra, Steve, and Tim were in the waiting room
the second day, along with other friends and Una,
John, and Jessie. There also was a man there nobody knew. Everybody thought somebody must
know him, or at least I knew him, or he wouldn't
have been there. He was wearing, as it was described to me later, a rather colorful running suit,
and he had "strange hair." I'm not certain what
strange hair looks like, but perhaps he'd just come
from nuclear medicine.

The doctors had been in and briefed everyone,
and, again, the prognosis wasn't a good one. The
whole thing had deteriorated into a death watch.

"I'm still not sure who brought it up," Dedra said, "but somebody said, 'Maybe we ought to pray.' So the guy in the running suit stands up and says, 'That's a wonderful idea, and I would be glad to lead you in a word.'

"We thought maybe he was some sort of minister you knew. Anyway, this man launches into the longest prayer you've ever heard. He goes on and on and on, and pretty soon it's evident he's some kind of nut who doesn't know you or anybody else in the room. He just sort of wandered in there.

"So, when he finally finished, everybody is pretty embarrassed, and the room is very quiet. Suddenly, Jessie looks up and asks him, 'You didn't come in here from Waco, did you?'

"It broke us all up. It really helped a lot."

I'm not certain where Jessie gets all her information sometimes, but if she has any, she will, in fact, share it. At one point during all this, she said to Dedra, "I heard Lewis gave you a ring."

"Yes, he did," Dedra replied, and showed it to my aunt.

"Well," said Jessie, "after his first operation, he was so mean his third wife couldn't live with him and had to leave."

Steve said, "There were some people that really went ballistic during all this, and it was scary. We didn't know which end was up half the time. So I'm sitting there, and everybody in talking and crying, and I see Jessie sitting by herself.

"I said, 'Aunt Jessie, are you all right?' "

"She said, 'I'm fine. If it's Lewis's time to go, all

these doctors and everything they have in this hospital and all this commotion isn't going to save him. But I just don't think it's his time yet.' "

Lord, what I must have put my friends and family through, though. Some of them canceled important out-of-town business trips to be at the hospital. Grown men's wives said their husbands cried like babies.

Bobby Entrekin said, "When it looked like you weren't going to make it, I went outside in my backyard one night and I prayed for you. I said, 'Lord, just give ol' Lewis one more chance.' About that time, the wind came up from nowhere and started blowing the trees back and forth. I know I was emotional, but it was like I had an answer."

Dudley and Danny both came to the hospital and kept the vigil. Another friend from out-of-town said of them, "I'd heard you talk about them, but I want to tell you something, partner. Those two boys love you. They fought tears the whole time."

James Shannon works for me. He does some driving and just generally handles things. James, who was at my house looking after my dog, Catfish, the black lab, decided if I saw Catfish, it might bring me around.

So James drove Catfish to Emory Hospital. He parked, got out of the car with the dog on a leash, walked into Emory, got on an elevator, and walked out onto the fourth floor, where the ICU is located. Catfish, a *very* large, black dog, saw a nurse and lost it.

"He started barking, and I couldn't make him

stop," said James. "I was going to try to sneak him
into your room. I thought it might make you better.
But I knew that nurse wouldn't let me in, so when
Catfish blew it for us, I got out of there. I figured
they'd have put both of us in jail."

☞ ♥ ☜

THURSDAY, March 25.

They managed to arouse me a bit. I opened my
eyes, in other words. I didn't say anything, but I
opened my eyes. They gave me another one of those
transesophageal echos (tube down my throat). I was
too drugged to protest. My left ventricle worked at 20
percent. My right at 10 percent.

The chronology reports, "Right foot becomes pale
during PM. No evidence of embolism."

FRIDAY, March 26.

I'm still arousable. And my kidney function is
better. I go back on the transplant list. Here, it gets
a little sticky.

Okay, I drink and smoke. We've been over that.
So what the doctors want to know is, if I were to
have a heart transplant, would I be willing to
change my lifestyle? That's apparently the deal
these days and is really the only thing that angers
me about all this.

Some doctors in England are now refusing to do
bypass surgeries on patients who smoke. Isn't this
a little God-playing here? It's the old Lifestyle Po-

lice again. Everybody wants to tell everybody else
how to live these days.

I certainly was in no shape to answer for myself,
but do you mean if my family or friends had said,
"No, I don't think that lowlife Lewis would change
his lifestyle if you had to save his life by giving him
a new heart," then it wouldn't have been done and
I would have died there because I might continue
my bad habits? What does the Hippocratic oath say
about that?

Doctors give good advice. Doctors don't want people to get sick and die. But should they be allowed
to pick who will live and who will die based on the
way they think patients ought to live?

We know that a poor diet can cause cholesterol,
which can cause blockage of coronary arteries.
They do bypass surgery for that, too. So, can a doctor say, "That person eats too many fried foods, so
let the grease-sucking son of a bitch just die?"

How about fat people?

"I'm not going to waste my time operating on
that fat fool. He should have lost weight so he
wouldn't have been in this condition."

And exercise is supposed to help prevent heart
disease. So might a doctor ask, "Does this person
jog?" And when told, "No, he doesn't," might he
then say, "Well, then I'm not going to operate"?

How far could something like this go? Would a
nondrinking doctor decide not to set somebody's
broken arm because that person got drunk and fell
down? Would a doctor refuse assistance to an auto-

accident victim because the patient was driving over the speed limit?

This could become a huge issue in the future. My answer to it is that any doctor who would refuse medical treatment because of a patient's lifestyle ought to be dragged out and flogged.

But back to my case. Everybody said, "We'll make that lowlife Lewis stop drinking and smoking and eating his favorite foods if you need to give him a new heart to keep him alive." That's sure as hell what I would have said. If you've been married as many times as I have, you know something about making promises you aren't at all sure you're going to be able to keep.

A heart transplant? Such a thing certainly had never entered my mind as a possibility before the surgery, and my doctors probably hadn't considered it, either. They certainly didn't mention it to me if they did.

When they mentioned it to some of my friends at the hospital, however, that's when there were a few lighter moments.

Knowing my love for Georgia and my hatred for rival Georgia Tech, not to mention my reputation for being homophobic, somebody said, "Doc, just don't give him a Tech lesbian's heart."

Dedra said a doctor looked out the window late Friday evening and—I guess thinking it was perfect conditions for a car crash—said, "It's Friday night, and it's raining. We might get a heart tonight."

SATURDAY, March 27.

The roller pumps must come out.

"We're still worried about infections at this point," said Dr. Martin, "and these things can cause them. Plus, nobody's ever been on them as long as you have without either suffering brain damage or dying."

The pumps were removed. Nobody knows what will happen. I'm still in a horrible state.

"You'd had so much fluids and drugs," I was told, "you wouldn't have even known yourself, your face and body were so bloated."

My heart started beating again when the pumps came out. Then it started beating even better. I was able to maintain my blood pressure on my own.

Praise the Lord and pass the morphine.

"But," explained Dr. Martin, "you were by no means out of the woods. You were still on the respirator (breathing device), the infection possibility was still there, and you were barely arousable, so the brain-damage possibility remained."

SUNDAY, March 28.

I'm still on the respirator, which is doing my breathing for me. Temperature down. Femoral-artery balloon removed.

MONDAY, March 29.

It's been a week. (But I'm still here.) Bad news:

"We find out you do have a fungus," Dr. Martin said. "We're still not sure you're going to make it."

It goes on. The fungus is identified as *Candida*

albicans, which sounds like a hockey team or a stripper. My right index finger has developed a dark tip. So has the little finger on my right hand. Probably blood clots.

On Thursday, April 1, they were able to take my breathing tube out. I could even talk.

"After that, we were *really* worried about brain damage," said my doctor.

"You were totally out of it. You were seeing Winston Churchill in the paper towels across from your bed. We'd noticed your legs, too. They were mottled, red and white all over. We figured if your legs were in that kind of shape, what would your brain look like?"

But on the chronology, under April 5—two weeks after the surgeries—the following appears: "Old self?"

Dr. Martin explained that:

"Steve, Dudley and I were in your room. You were awake and trying to talk, but your words were terribly slurred. You actually were making us laugh. You were trying to tell us all about this and that, and we had no idea about anything you were saying.

"I said to them—figuring you wouldn't hear me or have any idea what I was talking about—'He sounds like that guy who plays the drunk on television.'

"Steve and Dudley knew who I was talking about, but the three of us could not recall his name. Now, keep in mind, we still don't know what the situation is with your brain yet, and you sound like you could have some speech problems and that you may not have managed to maintain all your mental capabilities.

"So we're trying our best to think of this guy's name, and out of the blue, you say, 'Foster Brooks.' We all felt like cheering. There were the three of us who couldn't muster up his name from anywhere, and you got it."

My heart is working again. My kidneys are, too. There's the fungus, but I can remember Foster Brooks when three people standing up can't.

"I was really encouraged now," said Dr. Martin. "We all started breathing a little easier."

The very next day, I developed hemorrhoids.

★★★ 7 ★★★

THE WAY I FIGURE IT, IT WAS WEDNESDAY, APRIL 7, when I came back to the real world after being out of it for nearly three weeks. I'll go into the places I went, the things I saw, and the deeds I did in my drugged brain later.

Foster Brooks really hadn't been that difficult. It was a throwaway, like, "Who started the first game of the '59 World Series for the White Sox?"

Easy. Early Wynn. The Dodgers won it, by the way, 11–0. *Eleven.*

But on that Wednesday, the chronology says that my speech was less slurred and that I was sitting up in my bed in the intensive-care unit. It also says the following:

"Peed on Dr. Martin's shoes after warning Dr. Martin he had to pee."

That's what I did, and they put it right there in the chronology for medical history to see it for the rest of eternity.

At some point, I would like to sit down with a psychologist to see if I could unearth all the deep-seated reasons I peed on Dr. Martin's shoes, but, for now, I will have to go just with the obvious ones.

And allow me to point out, and it's in the historical record, I didn't pee on Dr. Martin's shoes without warning him first. Well, I didn't warn him I was actually going to pee on his shoes, but I did warn him I had to pee. If he had been a dentist, I would simply have just hung turk, as we used to say, with no warning, and let it fly right there on his Guccis, bought, I am certain, with all that pain money from root canals and Novocain shots to the eyeballs.

But Dr. Martin had been kind to me, so I said, "Dr. Martin, I have to pee."

Then I just sort of rolled over in my bed, took matters in hand, and had at it. Right on top of his shoes. I think they were an attractive pair of loafers. I don't think they were Guccis, however. When Guccis are hit by a liquid, I have noticed, the liquid tends to bead a little more than it did on Dr. Martin's shoes.

He jumped back and said, "You've peed on my shoes."

I said, "That's for the fifteen (at least) tubes."

I do suppose it was a partially revenge-motivated move. I mean, these people had done things to me I wouldn't have done to a rabid dog. I realize they were trying to keep me alive, but they will *hurt* you in a hospital. I missed a great deal of it, of course, but Dr. Martin, after all, had been the one to order the first transesophageal echo when I had to swallow that garden hose.

I guess peeing on his shoes was also an attempt to get back at all those bloodsuckers over the years who stuck me with a thousand needles, for the isotopes, for the catheters, for the times I've heard, "This may sting a little" and, seconds later, was looking for a place to land.

And now that I am totally lucid, I think of all the other shoes I wished I'd peed on over the years. There are several lawyers I would have liked to have hosed down. I would have gone for their socks, too, if the truth be known. I already mentioned dentists. I would have gone right up to their knees. And a few auto mechanics who charged me seven hundred dollars to repair something that wasn't working again the next day, and everybody who gets in the passing lane of an interstate and goes eleven miles an hour. *Eleven.*

Regardless, the fact is, I was thinking mean again, which in this instance was good news because it meant my brain was in about the same shape it was in before my ordeal. Dr. Martin, incidentally, summoned one of his medical students to clean off his shoes, and there might be a new pair of Bally of Switzerland on my medical bill, but I dare anybody to try to find it.

I was cooking now. Nobody had sat down with me and explained just how close I had come to dying—

and that I was still a very sick individual—so I didn't have any of that to concern me. I just knew I was in a hospital, that my surgery was over, and then, for the first time, I noticed there was a television above my bed. I didn't actually watch it, but I did see it was there and made a mental note to check it out later to see if the guy in the coffee commercial had gotten into that woman's knickers while I'd been away.

THURSDAY, April 8.

The chronology reads, "Intermittently confused." I wasn't seeing Winston Churchill in the paper towels anymore. I was seeing Bill Clinton.

FRIDAY, April 9.

"Right chest tube removed." I was aware of that. The guy who removed my right chest tube said, "This may sting a little." It didn't sting at all. It hurt like a son of a bitch. Not for long, but for the entire .002 seconds it took him to yank out the tube from my chest, it hurt beyond belief. I tried to pee on his shoes, but I missed. He was too quick. A veteran, this guy.

SATURDAY, April 10.

"Low grade fever."

SUNDAY, April 11.

This was the day I made it all the way back. I will tell you how it happened:

The day began with a visit from my friend Bob

Dunn from Orlando. I play a lot of golf with Bob, a
native Georgian who is also a huge Bulldog fan.
Bob was in my room, and he apparently had seen
me earlier when I was in my expanded state.

"Damn if you don't look a whole lot better," he
said. "You'll be out of here in no time and will be
whipping my ass on the golf course again."

Bob is a modest man. He carries the best ten
handicap I know. I always win with him. I rarely
win against him. Bob and I are both members of
the lovely Lake Nona Golf Club in Orlando. Once,
a group of Brits came to Lake Nona to play our
team. While he was visiting, Bob even brought up
my match against a knight. I actually played a guy
named "Sir Something-or-other," and I didn't know
what to call him.

Bob was laughing. "You referred to him as 'Your
Highness' a couple of times, and even, 'Nice shot,
Your Majesty.'"

Believe it or not, I remembered exactly what I
said to him when I closed him out on the fifteenth
hole.

I said, "Good knight."

Bob left.

A nurse was monkeying around with my I.V.
tank, which was still dripping in a clear liquid that
was either an antibiotic, a drug, or new clear Tab
for all I knew, when I noticed the television again.
I heard these two words and looked up.

"Amen Corner."

Yes! I knew what they meant. The Amen Corner
is what all of golf calls the eleventh, twelfth, and

thirteenth holes at the hallowed Augusta National Golf Club.

"What day is it?" I asked the nurse.

"Sunday," she said.

"I knew that," I replied, "I just wanted to make sure you did."

The nurse didn't laugh.

By God, it was the final day of the Masters! That's why Bob Dunn had come by. He was on his way to Augusta, 120 miles east of Atlanta, for the final round of the Masters golf tournament at Augusta National.

I'd missed the first fifty-four holes of the tournament! That hadn't happened to me for nearly forty years. I'd been to the Masters and covered it for four different newspapers, and here it was the final day, and I didn't even know who was leading.

I stared at the TV screen. I had no idea where my eyeglasses were, and neither did the humorless nurse, so the image on the screen wasn't completely clear. I could see a lot of green. I knew that was the grass. And there was white and pink. That would be the dogwoods and azaleas.

"I need you to do something for me," I said to the nurse.

"Okay," she said, "but just don't pee on my shoes."

Word travels fast in a hospital.

"Watch that screen," I said, "and see if you can find out who's leading the Masters."

"Who are the masters?" she asked.

Why me?

As it turned out, the nurse didn't have to help me. Suddenly, I heard Pat Summerall of CBS say that the leader was Bernhard Langer of Germany and that Chip Beck of Fayetteville, North Carolina, who had played his college golf at the University of Georgia and who was an acquaintance of both Bob Dunn's and mine, was in hot pursuit of him as they entered the Amen Corner.

I discovered if I squinted my eyes, I actually could see a lot of what was going on on the television.

A word here:

I'm a pretty patriotic fellow. And in any sort of conflict, sporting or otherwise, I pull for the Americans against any foreigners. There has only been one exception to that. The Soviet national basketball team came over and played Georgia Tech in Atlanta once, and I pulled for the Russians.

But I certainly pull for Americans in golf, and it remains a great sense of pride to me that in my only international match to date—the one against the Brits at Lake Nona—I won. The last thing I wanted to see on this Sunday was for a goddamned German (who had won the tournament before, incidentally) to beat out Chipper Beck and win another green jacket, which is awarded the Masters champion along with that big check.

My squinted eyes were riveted, as they say, to the television screen.

They played ten and then entered the Amen Corner. Come on, Chip. I figured disaster on the par-4 eleventh, but nothing happened. Then they went on through the treacherous par-3 twelfth, and Chip was still close. The par-5 thirteenth was next, and here is where Chip gets this Nazi, I thought to myself. He can reach in two shots, maybe make the putt for eagle, and catch Herr Langer.

It didn't happen. It was Herr Langer who eagled. Chip was in a great deal of trouble. Another nurse came into my room and tried to get me to take some medicine.

"Tell Dr. Mengele I won't be taking any more of his medicine," I said to her.

The par-5 fifteenth was Chip's last chance. I knew it. Pat Summerall, Ken Venturi, Ben Wright, and Gary McCord of CBS knew it. The Masters gallery knew it. The vast television audience knew it. The nurse who wanted to know who the masters were and Chip Beck were the only two people who didn't know it.

Chip *had* to go for the green in two. He had to make an eagle 3 to catch the blond German. The two golfers hit their tee shots. Both were okay.

There is a small pond in front of the fifteenth green at Augusta. Some golfers, trying to reach the green in two, have landed in that pond and shot their way out of Masters contention. But it was Chip Beck's only chance. He had to pull out a fairway wood, ignore the pond, and blast away.

But he didn't. He pulled out a short iron and laid up in front of the pond.

"No, Chip, no!" I shouted.

Nurses came running into the room.

"Are you okay?" one asked.

"Hell, no!" I shouted. "Can't you see what's happening here? Chip Beck is giving in to a German! My own father fought through the hedgerows of France to beat these sons of bitches, and here's a Georgia Bulldog laying up!"

Somebody went to get me a pill.

Just as everybody knew would happen, Chip lost any chance of winning with his decision at fifteen, and, before the pill took effect and I went to sleep, I had to lie there in that hospital bed and watch them put another green jacket on Field Marshal Langer. I felt worse about this than I did when Toronto beat Atlanta in the 1992 World Series. At least Canada fought on our side during World War II, and I will eventually get around even to forgiving them for introducing hockey to this country.

Still, I was back. All the way. From that moment on, I was clearheaded and knew all that was going on around me. I even began to pick up on the events of the previous three weeks. I didn't try to deal with any of it yet. I still had the hemorrhoidal condition, for one thing, which is enough to deal with, what with the pain and embarrassing and irritating itch.

On Monday, April 12, twenty-two days after the surgery, they finally moved me to a room outside the intensive-care unit. They don't move you out of ICU unless they no longer think you could croak at any minute. But I was still a sick man, and the problem with being fully aware after such an ordeal as I went through is you now know what all is going on around you. Thus, you have to deal with certain situations that occur for each and every patient who goes through postoperative care in a hospital, intensive care or no intensive care. I will be brief regarding the most obvious ones:

- There is no way to lie in bed comfortably because everything hurts. Everything.
- I had a VCR in my room, but Dedra couldn't find any movies I hadn't already seen, and Emory didn't have cable, so I had to watch *Donahue* one day. They were interviewing people who had had sex with goats, I seem to recall. The Folger's couple was included, by the way.
- It's hard to get any good sleep because nurses awaken you to give you sleeping pills, on top of the fact you can't get comfortable in the bed.
- You have to deal with food. Veteran that I was, I knew better than to try to eat any of the hospital food, all of which is poisonous, but I even had trouble eating the outside food Dedra brought in for me. Before, they fed you intravenously. But now, I had to try to get down nourishment through my mouth. Nothing tasted good to me except green seedless grapes—I must have eaten a thousand green, seedless grapes. I saw Ernest and Julio Gallo in the paper towels one night.
- I asked if James could bring Catfish to see me. They laughed.

There are other dilemmas, however, that might not be quite as obvious to those who have never gone through this experience. Some are rather personal, to be sure, but I will, as I promised, attempt to be as delicate as possible.

Everybody knows about hospital gowns. They have no back to them. I explained earlier that this is to make it very uncomfortable for the patient while lying on a cold steel table. It is also so they can give you a shot in your butt quickly and get a bedpan in the correct position before any sort of accident can take place that gives a hospital laundry room fits.

The problem with a man wearing a gown, however, is that most men don't wear gowns at any other time except when they are in hospitals. Men who wear gowns at other times march in a lot of parades these days, but this is no time to go into that.

What a gown does when being worn in a hospital bed is ride up. With no tugging involved whatsoever, it just sort of rides up when you aren't looking. You don't wear any underwear under your gown in a hospital, so, to be perfectly blunt about it, the whole world gets a number of shots at your testicles.

I didn't mean for anybody to have a look at my testicles, but it just happened. I would kick my covers off, my gown would ride up, and Dedra would say, "For God's sake, Lewis, pull your gown down. Everybody can see your testicles."

To be perfectly honest about it, I really didn't care if anybody saw my testicles. The nurses, for instance. Imagine how many testicles they had already seen over their careers. It's something they ask all nursing candidates as they enter nursing school.

"You aren't getting into this line of work just so you can see testicles, are you?"

All nurses answer, "Of course not." I imagine some are lying, but they usually wind up working in sperm banks. I actually talked to a nurse once who worked for a urologist; she said she would peek through the door to watch men masturbate into condoms when they had to have their sperm checked. (I'm sorry. I was supposed to be delicate, wasn't I?)

It doesn't take you long in a hospital to lose most of your dignity, anyway. You check it at the admitting office.

"We'll take your dignity now," says the admitting nurse. "Just leave it right here on the desk. We'll give it back when you are discharged."

But I was embarrassed later when Dedra said that a minister came to see me with his wife, and she was one of those who got a free shot. Apparently, I also bared my testicles during a visit by a woman delivering flowers and balloons to my room. Not to mention that I'd flashed the entire hospital public-relations staff, who had visited me to beseech me not to give the *National Enquirer* the story about peeing on Dr. Martin's shoes.

"The entire staff?" I asked.

"All of them," said Dedra.

I would like to take this opportunity to apologize and ask the obvious question—when will medical science invent a suitable codpiece to avoid such situations?

Now that I have discussed showing my testicles, I figure just about anything goes, but I am still trying to remain soft core here:

Intensive care is bedpan alley. After you are released from there, you have to do it all in the rest room. You have to get out of your bed and walk (in my case, with a walker. I wasn't hoofing it that well as yet) into the rest room.

Number one is no problem whatsoever. Number two is. With all the cutting that was done on my chest, I didn't have a great deal of reach. Do I have to paint a clearer picture here? I think not.

Suddenly, you're four years old again and haven't learned your way around a roll of toilet paper. Mom did that for you, remember? You said, "Mom, I'm through," and in she came to finish things off.

You have to do that in the hospital after heart surgery, too. Imagine a forty-six-year-old man having to shout out, "I'm through," and in comes a nurse.

I didn't attempt to carry on a conversation with any of the nurses while any of this was taking place. I didn't think it was any time for chitchat, and I am certain they all appreciated that.

But I wondered to myself, Do they tell nurses—after they ask about the testicles—they might have to do this sort of thing following graduation?

If they do, I wonder just how many people get run out of nursing and go into demolition, upholstery repair, or selling aluminum siding as a result?

I hereby bow in behalf of and thank all nurses who had to do that to me while I was recuperating in Emory Hospital. As long as I am alive, yours is not a thankless task.

As long as I am discussing nurses, I must mention a special three. Lord knows how many of these good women (*and* a man or two) took care of me, but three in particular deserve specific mention.

There was nurse Mary. Nurse Mary took care of me after my first heart surgery, too, about which I also wrote a book. It is called *They Tore Out My Heart and Stomped That Sucker Flat*, and nurse Mary German is one of the people to whom I dedicated the book.

Nurse Mary was back this time. Not a kinder, gentler woman have I ever known. She rubbed my back, feet, and legs, which were in a particular amount of pain. She held my hand when I asked her to; she changed the channel of my hospital TV when I simply couldn't watch Geraldo interview people who had married their pets.

It was Mary German who wheeled me out of Emory Hospital when they finally let me go. Mary, I love you.

And nurse Gabby. I fell in love with my camp counselor when I was seven. I fell in love with nurse Gabby the same way. She was young and pretty and sweet and held my hand when they were checking my hemorrhoids. I love you, too, Gabby.

And then there was the physical-therapy nurse. I don't know her name. I'm not going to try to find out her name. I don't even remember the physical-therapy nurse, but I was told about her, and what I am trying to do here is to avoid a lawsuit by the physical-therapy nurse.

"She couldn't have been nicer to you," Dedra said, "but you hated her. For some reason, you hated this woman."

I had been lying around there in a hospital bed for weeks, and that's not good for your muscles. I don't have a lot of muscle development to begin with, and what I had went even limper during those weeks.

So they brought in this physical-therapy nurse, I was told, to try to get me to do a few simple movements to keep things as flexible and strong as was possible.

Apparently, I didn't want to do any of these movements.

"Apparently?" said Dedra. "You made this poor woman's life miserable. Whenever she would walk into the room, you would scream, 'Get her away from me!' You cussed her and called her names and even tried to hit her. Fortunately, you didn't have the strength to do anybody any physical harm."

I honestly don't remember any of this. I do recall dreaming once about Cordie Mae Poovey, a girl in my hometown who could beat up every boy in school, not to mention several men in town, including both the Baptist and Methodist preachers and the town drunk, Curtis (Fruit Jar) Haney.

Cordie Mae later married Hog Philpott. Cordie

Mae went at least 220, and Hog doubled her. Pound for pound, it was the biggest wedding in county history. Later, after Hog lost his job at the Atlanta and West Point Railway Depot in Moreland when the trains stopped running, Cordie Mae began a career as a female professional wrestler to make ends meet. She wrestled as the Masked Turnip and won several title belts. She was barred from the ring forever one night in Sylacauga, Alabama, however, after not only maiming her female opponent but breaking the arm of the referee and bloodying the noses of six male spectators who tried to rip off her mask.

In my dream, I was back in the fourth grade, and Mrs. Summers, our teacher, had us out on the playground teaching us to do the Virginia reel. As Cordie Mae came down the line, she grabbed my hand and slung me off my feet. I landed in a large patch of kudzu fifty yards away. I suppose I thought the physical-therapy nurse was Cordie Mae Poovey, and she was either trying to dance with me, break my arm, bloody my nose, or get me in her famous Eye Gouge Hold, later banned by the International Wrestling Federation.

So, I apologize to the physical-therapy person. I am not a violent man and never have been. And tell your lawyers if they try to sue me, I'll pee on their socks.

Damn, I wanted to go home. The days passed, and I would have done anything to get out of Emory Hospital, despite the fact everybody was doing his or her best to make me as comfortable as possible.

Somebody made certain I had a newspaper every morning. The Braves were off to a bad start. The president was trying to get gays in the military. A doctor said, "If that son of a bitch has his way, 'closing ranks' is going to have a whole new meaning in the military."

One thing I do like about doctors is most of them are conservative like me.

Hillary was working on reforming the health-care system. Guess how doctors feel about that?

It was the newspaper that caused me to notice the only mental defect I might have had because of all that had happened. I'm a crossword-puzzle worker. I know that a "pother" is a "stir" and that the answer to the clue "courage" can be "sand."

When those newspapers started coming to me in the hospital, I couldn't do the puzzle. I might get one or two words, but that was about it. I was quite concerned about that.

"You'll be lucky," said Dr. Martin, "if everything about you is back to normal in six months."

Dr. Martin was especially kind to me during this period. He even took me for strolls outside the hospital in my wheelchair.

"We ought to take Dedra or a nurse with us," I finally said to him. "People may start to talk."

But here was a busy man, a doctor, who was taking the time to push me around the Emory campus and get me out of a hospital room. Late one beautiful April day, we were outside, and I asked him to stop my chair near a lovely bed of tulips.

I'm certain I broke fourteen hundred campus laws and committed a horrid discretion gardeners would have wanted to shoot me for, but I reached over and plucked one of those tulips out of the bed and took it back to my room with me.

I think it was the very first flower I ever picked. It just seemed like the thing to do at the time. Later, when Aunt Jessie came to visit me, I hid the tulip. I had placed it in a vial of water. For all I knew, she could have planted that tulip bed, and I was in no shape to be worn out by my eightyish aunt.

But I still wanted to go home. I wanted to see my dog. This was the second operation he'd gone through with me. No woman can claim that.

I had to blow and suck into and out of a tube twice a day for my breathing exercises. An I.V. was still in, and the bloodsuckers kept coming. They took blood every day to see how the blood thinner was working. I took large pills. Many large pills. I spent a lot of time talking to lots of doctors who were still doing a lot of looking at me and poking at me.

"Does this hurt?" they would ask after a poke.

I never know what to say in that situation.

If it does hurt, and I say, "No," they might leave me alone, but if it hurts and I say, "No," then they also might not do anything to make it stop hurting.

But if it hurts, and I say, "Yes," then God knows what sort of procedure I might face.

To be on the safe side, I always answered, "I hurt everywhere," and then begged for a pain pill.

There were stitches that had to come out, too. Those little suckers *do* sting when they are pulled.

And there was much conversation about the tip of my right index finger.

The cardiology people brought in orthopedic people and plastic-surgeon people to look at it because it had turned dark black, probably because of a blood clot. The tip of my right little finger was also black, but it was judged to be on the road to recovery.

They wanted to chop off the tip of my right index finger.

"We'll deaden your entire hand," said the orthopedic guy.

The plastic-surgeon guy said he could put a prosthesis on the end of the finger after the tip had been chopped off.

"Nobody messes with my finger," I said.

I wasn't going to have another operation anytime soon. It was that simple.

Again, Dr. Martin came to my rescue.

"I say we just wait and see what happens," was his suggestion.

If my tulip hadn't died, I'd have given it to him right there.

There was also much discussion about my finger from visiting friends. It usually began with, "What in the hell happened to your finger?"

"Blood clot," I would tell them, "but it could have gone to my brain."

"Could have gone to your dick, too," said one.

☞ ♥ ☜

Obviously, when a patient has been in the shape I had been in for such a long time, there is reluctance to allow the patient to leave the hospital. There is reluctance to allow a patient to leave the hospital anyway. That's one less body to play on.

But there finally came that day when the doctors agreed I could, in fact, go home. I had to make a lot of promises, like I wouldn't go on a three-week drinking binge to celebrate or I wouldn't try my hand at rodeoing.

But I don't think there really is any way to get well in a hospital. You can get better, but you can't get well. There's that hospital smell, for instance. They spray that stuff, whatever it is, around, so if you aren't sick when you walk in, you'll be sick soon enough.

I already mentioned the poisonous food in a hospital (If it's white, it's a nurse. If it's red, it's blood. If it's gray, it's the food. So that's where they get the meat in the Soviet Union).

And people are always doing things for you in a hospital, and I'm the kind of person who, if somebody will do it for me, I won't try to do it for myself (see toilet problems, on previous pages).

I needed to get out of there. Get in my own bed. Sit on my own back porch and listen to the birds and watch Catfish chase the squirrels and get a little sun, for God's sake.

I got out on April 17.

I had walked into Emory Hospital on March 21. I didn't walk out. But, as I mentioned, nurse Mary German did roll me out of there on a wheelchair on Saturday, April 17. I had been a patient for twenty-seven days. I had been to death's door and back out of it.

Nurse Mary took me down the elevator and out the emergency exit. I was wearing a running suit, a pair of bedroom slippers, and a University of Georgia baseball cap, the fitted wool version, not one of those pretender hats with the plastic strap in the back so one size can fit all. This is no time to launch into a long discussion about what went wrong with hats in this country, but may whoever thought of that plastic strap be beset by a physical-therapy nurse who looks like Cordie Mae Poovey with a bad hangover.

There was press there. Microphones. Television cameras. I didn't say anything. I was helped into Dedra's Cherokee Jeep van, and she drove me toward home.

On the way, we stopped for a curb service at Atlanta's famous Varsity Restaurant, which, I think I read somewhere, serves more hamburgers and chili dogs than any other place on the planet. I ordered one chili dog, french fries, and a frosted orange. That's orange juice mixed with ice cream. I got only half the chili dog down, but I finished the rest of my order.

But I had done something normal. I was out of

the hospital, and I had stopped at a fast-food restaurant. I don't know how others have begun their post-operative recoveries, but I went for chili dogs and fries. I was proud of myself.

"See if there's a rodeo in town," I said to Dedra as we drove away from the Varsity.

I was kidding. She wasn't sure.

I would still be on 416 different medicines. I would have to have home nursing care, and Dedra rented a hospital bed for my house. But I wouldn't have to wear a gown, so I was through showing my testicles for a while. Everything still hurt. Catfish was glad to see me, and I was glad to see him.

I weighed 146 pounds. I'm six-one. I had lost fourteen pounds off the very slight frame I had checked into the hospital.

I had no diet restrictions.

"Eat anything you want," Dr. Martin had told me. "Just gain some weight."

But the experience of the past month still hadn't sunk in completely. That must be how it is for a lot of patients who have been critically ill. The present—the lingering pain and discomfort, the readjustment to home—overshadows all that.

What had happened to me would come later, mostly in bits and pieces. The doctors would fill me in, of course, as would Dedra and Steve, who had been there for every step. And I would get little stories and anecdotes from friends who visited.

There were two other elements involved, too. First there was the matter of just how I managed to survive when practically everybody involved had thought I had no chance. Something saved me. What was it? What procedure, what lifesaving maneuver, what experimental drug, had kept me alive and had allowed me to leave Emory Hospital still among the quick?

And I had to answer that question that has been coming up over and over since I left the hospital:

"What's it like to nearly die?"

Gather close. This is the best part.

*** 8 ***

I WOULDN'T EVEN ATTEMPT TO TRY TO NAME ALL THE
narcotics I was given at Emory. Dr. Martin had
said, "We gave you all the drugs there were in
Georgia . . . and had feelers out to other states."

I know about the morphine. I'd had morphine before.

I used to talk about being in the hospital and "re-
laxing with a jar of morphine."

God bless morphine. It is named, of course, for
the good God of sleep, Morpheus: ". . . encrusted in
the arms of Morpheus." Did Shakespeare write
that? I didn't, but I could have.

Whatever the drugs were, they kept me in the
Land of Out to Lunch for days upon days, and the
answer to "What is it like to nearly die?" is this:

In my case, at least, there was no pain, no fear, no dread. If I had died at Emory, they could have written, "He died a peaceful death."

They could have written, "He wouldn't have known it if he'd been run over by a Roto-Rooter van" and would also have been correct.

No, I didn't have any out-of-body experiences, either. And I didn't see any bright lights. (I've already used this a hundred times, but my first attempt at humor following ICU was with a reporter from the *Atlanta Journal-Constitution*. I told her I had indeed seen a bright, beautiful light and had followed it, but it turned out to be a K-mart tire sale.) (K-mart stock went down soon after that, incidentally.)

I didn't see the face of God, unfortunately. I didn't hear any angels singing. They were too busy watching over me to sing. But I didn't smell anything sulfurous, either, for that matter.

What I did was rest in peace and dream. Did I dream! I dreamed things that I can't believe I'm actually going to write down in this book. I don't mind relating how I showed my testicles to the Western world and couldn't take care of the process necessary following a bowel movement, but I had some strange dreams, and when I describe them, there will be those who will utter the immortal words that are a punch line to a joke (speaking of goats), "Damn, brother, don't believe I would have told that."

There is still the matter of peeing on the doctor's shoes to take up with a psychologist, and I guess

one day I also should get around to having somebody see if he could interpret some of these dreams
for me. Then again, maybe I don't want to know.

But before I begin, there ought to be a little background here about a part of me that probably could
fill psychiatric volumes.

I would have liked to have been a soldier. No real
puzzle there. My father was one. He was in the in-
fantry. He received a battlefield commission during
World War II. He also received the Bronze Star for
bravery and a Purple Heart. My father also served
in Korea. Two wars were too much for him, and the
army didn't help him, and he died young.

For the first six years of my life, I lived on a military base. The memories I have of my father are
mostly those in which he is wearing the uniform.

My heart condition kept me out of military service. I knew men who died in Vietnam. I have been
to the wall and touched their names.

Is there guilt because of my father's service and
the service of my peers and the lack of any on my
part?

Of course there is. I still feel there is only one ul-
timate gut check in life. And this is combat. An
older man once said to me:

"I was in the service during Korea, but I wasn't
sent over. And I still wonder about myself. I don't
care what else you know about yourself, unless
you've been there, you'll never know if you just
might turn tail and run the first moment you're in
combat."

I've now had three heart surgeries and three

marriages. But I still don't know if I've got any real courage.

I suppose that because of all this, I am keenly interested in military history, especially that of World War II. I'm the person who orders those videotapes featuring biographies of World War II figures off television.

I'd rather watch a World War II black-and-white documentary on A&E than the Playboy Channel.

I've read three biographies of Hitler, *The Rise and Fall of the Third Reich*, everything the brilliant Gordon Prange and John Toland have out about the war, and I've seen *Patton* two dozen times, and I own a print of perhaps one of the most extraordinary photographs ever taken in World War II.

Several years back, I was in Sausalito, California, and happened upon a shop advertising sporting and history photographs. I went inside. It was astounding. My entire childhood was in that shop.

There actually was a team photograph of the 1959 White Sox. There was a picture of Arnold Palmer winning at Augusta and photographs of two of my other sporting heroes, Don Drysdale and Sandy Koufax of the Dodgers. I bought those to hang on my wall, along with a picture of General George Patton standing next to a tank during World War II.

I wrote a column about these photographs, and several weeks later I received a letter from a man in North Carolina who had served with Patton. In the letter, he wrote that Patton had sworn that when he reached the Rhine, he was going to "piss in the Führer's river."

The man sent me a print of General George Patton pissing, indeed, in the Führer's river during the Allied crossing of the Rhine into Germany. Given the chance, I'm certain old Blood n' Guts would have pissed on Hitler's shoes, too.

I've read Herman Wouk's *Winds of War* and *War and Remembrance*, and I have tapes of the mini-series made from both books. Robert Mitchum, I must say, was a perfect Pug Henry. I still haven't forgiven the Japs for Pearl Harbor. Once a friend and I were at the shrine in Hawaii. A group of Japanese arrived and were taking pictures and laughing.

There were fifty of them. We were two. I will always regret we didn't charge.

Let me be perfectly honest here: If I could, I think I would now accept the opportunity to go back in time, and for it to be 1942 again and to be in the United States military and to be, preferably, fighting Nazis. It had to be one of the most incredible times to live in all of history.

Certainly, I could have had my guts blown, and it is easy to make such a pronouncement fifty years after the fact, but I really believe I would make such a choice.

I dreamed military dreams in the hospital. A lot of military dreams. That is what I have been leading up to here.

I usually was the hero in them. My father had been a hero. I covered his exploits in World War II

in a previous book. I don't care if my daddy blew up
Fort Benning after Korea, he was still my military
hero.

Simply to have worn the uniform once . . .

I dreamed at some point I was a young army
lieutenant in Italy. I was assigned to intelligence.
One day, the C.O. said, "Lieutenant Grizzard, you
are to report to General Eisenhower immediately."

I grabbed a jeep and went to Supreme Allied
Command Headquarters.

"Lieutenant," Ike said to me, "we have heard
from some of the Wehrmacht's high command that
many of Hitler's generals think there is no use continuing the war, that they know they are beaten.
The problem is, they must find a way to convince
Hitler of this. Can you help us?"

"You can count on me, General, sir," I replied.

With some help from the OSS, I was taken out of
the country and brought back to the States.

I caught a train from Washington (I love trains,
big in the forties, too) to New Mexico and immediately located the secret headquarters of the Manhattan Project, where scientists were at work
attempting to develop the atomic bomb.

"Let me have a picture of the bomb, a drawing,
anything," I said to the scientists.

One took out a pen and drew a big bomb on a
piece of cardboard he stripped off a box filled with
large rocks. I'm not sure of the significance of that,
but they were very large rocks.

I folded the piece of cardboard and put it under
the shirt of my uniform. I got back on the train,

rode it back to Washington, and then was flown back to Italy, where I immediately went to see General Eisenhower. I told him what I had.

"Tell the German generals to come in," he said to an aide.

Some German generals came in. I think one was Jodl.

"Okay, Lieutenant Grizzard," said Ike, "show 'em what you've got."

I reached under my shirt and pulled out the piece of cardboard.

"See this big bomb?" I said to the generals. "You take this back to the Führer and tell him if he doesn't surrender, we're going to drop it on him. And if that doesn't work, we've got a lot of really big rocks, too."

Hitler announced Germany's surrender shortly thereafter in my dream.

"You have ended the war a year early," Ike said to me as he was pinning on my medal.

I also dreamed I was a commander on a navy aircraft carrier in the Pacific during World War II. Somebody stole my strawberries, but I didn't care. I was too busy planning my next move against Yamamoto.

I may have been Ernie Pyle in a dream. I was a war correspondent. It was a frustrating dream. I was trying to type while pinned down by Nazi automatic arms fire, and the ribbon on my typewriter came off.

There were times after the surgery I was convinced I was a returning serviceman in a military hospital in Washington, D.C. Doctors even said they often asked me if I knew where I was. And I would answer, "Emory Hospital."

"And where is Emory?" they would ask further.

"Washington," I would tell them.

A former fiancée came to visit me. I didn't remember it, but when I was told about it later, I dimly recalled seeing her face and also recalled thinking at the time she was a June Allyson-type nurse.

Dr. Jones said he visited me one day and asked me if I wanted anything to eat.

"I'll have whatever General Patton is having," he said I answered him.

I would have one dream about my father.

When the Chinese entered the conflict in Korea, my father's outfit had been wiped out near the Yalu River. Only he and one other man survived. My father, then a captain, hid under the dead and managed to escape after the Chinese victors left the area.

He later was befriended by a Chinese soldier trying to defect to the United Nations forces. Neither knew where the friendly lines were located. The Chinese soldier hid my father in a small, cold cave for six weeks. He brought food every day and kept my father from being captured by the enemy that was all over the area. Both eventually made it back to the Americans.

The family used to mumble a lot about my daddy when I was in the room as a little boy. They knew he hadn't been the same after Korea. And my daddy had gotten into some kind of trouble with the army after he returned home. His brother, a lawyer, tried to help him but discovered Daddy had been borrowing a lot of money on base at Fort Benning, even from enlisted men, a serious infraction for an officer. The army eventually dismissed him as unfit from military duty, and I covered all of what happened after that in another book.

But everybody used to mumble, "I wonder what really happened to him?"

I heard my Uncle Dorsey, my mother's brother, wonder aloud once, when nobody thought I was listening, "You don't reckon he did anything wrong over there in Korea, do you?"

Nobody ventured an answer to that, but it made me wonder—what could Daddy have done wrong over there in Korea?

I was seven or eight. I asked an older friend who was ten or eleven, "What could a soldier do wrong in a war?"

"I don't know," said my friend. "Maybe give away secrets to the enemy."

Certainly, my daddy wouldn't have done anything like that, but this kid was a lot older than I and knew lots more than I did. We never did find out what went wrong with Captain Lewis McDonald Grizzard, Sr., and probably never will, but I had this dream in the hospital:

I met a woman. I'm not certain how I met her, but she appeared in my life from some unknown place, and she said to me, "There's a lot you would like to know about your daddy, isn't there?"

Naturally, I said there was.

She took me into a room. She closed the shades and cut down the lights. She opened a side door to the room, and there was a garage. In the garage sat a Lincoln Continental limousine, a cream-colored one. I would say it was a middle sixties model.

Two Orientals got out of the limousine and walked into the room. One was a man who appeared to be about my age. The other was a woman, who appeared to be a few years younger than I am. The man handed me what appeared to be a photo album.

I opened it. There were old photographs inside.

Every photograph was the same. It was my father in his uniform, with a young Oriental boy and girl at his knees.

The woman said, "Lewis, I want you to meet your half-brother and -sister."

They told me the story.

Daddy had been on a secret mission in North Korea. He had been captured, however, and had been sent to a North Korean prison camp, where he had been tortured unmercifully.

"But he never said anything," the Oriental woman, my half-sister (I didn't get any names), said to me in the dream.

Afterward, Daddy had been sent to a forced labor camp, where he had met a North Korean woman in the rice paddies where he worked.

The woman who had brought me to the room explained more.

"Your daddy was certain he would die in that

camp. He never thought he would see you or your mother ever again. And he was very lonely. He was as lonely as he had ever been in his life.

"This North Korean woman was good to him. She bandaged his bloody feet."

(My father's feet had been severely frostbitten in the cave. They bothered him the rest of his life. I can still recall there would be blood on his socks when he took his shoes off at night.)

"So," the woman went on, "your father had two children with the North Korean woman. He managed to escape, later, however, and could not take any of them with him. So, when he got home, he was afraid to tell anybody, and he had to send back lots of money to North Korea for his family there. That is what happened to your father."

I never did find out the significance of the limousine. And that was the end of my dream.

It will haunt me for the rest of my life.

☞ ♥ ☜

The more I think of it, the more I seem to have dreamed a lot about being a hero. Even in nonmilitary dreams, I was saving the day.

The University of Georgia was trying to sign a large basketball player from Mississippi. I was summoned to the office of athletic director Vince Dooley.

"You've got to help us sign this player," said Dooley. (Any alumni effort to help in recruiting is against recruiting rules. May the NCAA please take note here: This was just a dream.)

"This young man loves gospel music," Dooley went on, "and Ole Miss is bringing in Mahalia Jackson to sing for him at a private concert. You go and sing, too."

There's another connection with my father here. He was a great loyalist to gospel music and could sing it with anybody.

I went to the Mahalia Jackson appearance. When she was finished, I got up and sang "Precious Memories" to the recruit. He signed with Georgia immediately.

Another dream: There was a British Open tradition in effect for over a century that said the winner of this most prestigious golf tournament had to drink a special grog from his trophy to make his victory official. It was the eve of the final round, at the Old Course in St. Andrews, Scotland, however, and the recipe for the grog had been misplaced. Who do you think was called upon to find the recipe and save the Open?

I had to do some serious searching, but I probed the streets of St. Andrews—I had visited there twice since my aborted attempt after the Soviet Union—and located an old widow in a house at the end of an alley. I had to promise to get her two tickets to the Dinah Shore Open in Palm Springs, but she said she did have the recipe for the grog, and she gave it to me.

I took it back to Open officials, and we mixed up a batch. And a damn fine grog it was, too.

I, of course, can look into my past to find at least some references to most of the dreams. But I had a few that came God knows from where, or from what new experimental drug.

I dreamed a lot of water dreams. They told me later I was thirsty a great deal as I was coming out, which was normal.

In one dream, I was on an airplane that had landed in Guatemala. Nurse Gabby was on the plane with me. So was Steve. Then my Aunt Una and Uncle John came on the plane. I was told we were making a refueling stop. I asked Gabby to bring me some water. She said the water was bad in Guatemala, and it would make me sick.

I said I didn't care. I had to have water.

Aunt Una went outside the plane and talked to the pilot. He had some water in a thermos, and she brought it back to me. But the stewardess took it away.

"The people of Guatemala need this water," she said.

In another dream, Steve and I were in the military, but this was present time. We were on a plane that crashed in the desert. I was thirsty again. I went outside the plane to look for water. There was a stock-car race going on outside the plane. A guy gave me a beer.

In another dream, an Arab doctor was treating me in a house. I don't know whose house. Standing next to me was a sculpture of a large bird. I was thirsty. I kept begging the doctor for water. He wouldn't give me any. The bird said, "He's a rotten son of a bitch. He won't give me any water, either."

I dreamed I was at a horse race, and I was thirsty. I went down to the stables and drank out of one of the horse's pails.

I dreamed I was watching a basketball game being played outdoors on the banks of the Mississippi River. A guy came dribbling across the water and dunked the ball at one point during the game. I was thirsty again, so I decided to drink out of the river. By the time I got over to it, it had run dry.

☞ ♥ ☜

I wasn't going to tell about this dream. What the hell. I was on drugs.

There must have been doctors around me while I was having this dream. I'm certain there were.

In the dream, doctors are examining me. They take some blood and begin to analyze it.

"My God," said one. "Look at this."

The doctors crowded around. They mumbled and murmured, and then one said, "Look, it's got a head on it."

To get straight to this, doctors found a little figure in my blood. It had a little head, as they said.

"Woolly little head, isn't it?" a doctor mused.

They called nurse Gabby.

"Put this little figure in a bottle and take it to the lab right now," she was told.

Gabby went and got a bottle, a Windex bottle with Windex still in it. She put the little figure in the Windex, and he started swimming around in it. I guess it had gills.

Then she said to me, "Let's go."

I followed her. We went outside, and there was a train station. The lab was in another city.

"We'll have to wait for the train," she said. "It's running late."

Trains are always late in this country.

Gabby explained, "The doctors think they've discovered another gender," she said. "There are males like you and females like me, and they think this may be something else. It doesn't have a penis and doesn't have a vagina. It has a little hook. See?"

I looked into the bottle of Windex. The little figure did have a little hook for a private.

I remember her going to a soft-drink machine and bringing me a bottle of Mountain Dew at that point.

Then I noticed him. Know how Wyle E. Coyote looks after he's been run over by a truck in a Roadrunner cartoon—completely flat?

Well, there was this person attached to the wall of the train station, and he was completely flat.

I got the feeling he was trying to go unnoticed. I looked at the person again and all of a sudden recognized who it was. It was my friend Billy Anderson of Athens. We call him B.A.

"B.A.," I said to him. "You're flat."

He tried to ignore me.

"Gabby," I said, "I'd like you to meet my flat friend, B.A."

B.A. still didn't say anything.

"He's here to steal the bottle!" Gabby cried out.

"No, he's not," I assured her. "B.A. is a friend of mine."

I never did get B.A. to unflatten himself, speak, or come off that wall. When the train came, we boarded, and when we got off, we were back in Guatemala, and I was thirsty again.

I drank the bottle of Windex and swallowed whatever it was that was in there.

B.A. showed up, no longer flat, and started laughing at me.

"You swallowed a queer." He laughed.

Gabby, naturally, was outraged and said she didn't love me anymore. B.A. thought that was funny, too.

My personal interpretation of this dream has to do with the fact they're pushing this idiot gender-equality thing with colleges these days, and Georgia might eventually have to give up football scholarships so the damn coeds can have a field-hockey team. I'd rather watch little whatevers play water polo in a bottle of Windex.

☞ ♥ ☜

I must admit I still feel some guilt regarding the fact I put family and friends through a lot while I dreamed away and, for the most part, had exciting, adventurous dreams. I have even had people say to me since, "Do you know what you put us through?"

And the answer must be, "No."

Maybe I should have hurt more. Maybe I should have been sweating it out with everybody else.

I heard stories of grown men crying for me, and I felt embarrassed. I heard stories of what some sacrificed in order to be with me. More guilt.

I mentioned this to the doctor.

"Just remember," he said, "that's what drugs are for."

Indeed.

☞ ♥ ☜

I wasn't finished with Emory Hospital. After I got home, I still had a million miles to go to recover. Every inch of my chest hurt. I could barely stand a shirt over it. My legs were so weak, I could barely walk without Dedra on my arm. I was sick of grapes and ate so much ice cream one day, I got sick of that.

A nurse showed up twice a day to take my blood to check the blood thinner. She was one of the best bloodsuckers I've ever had. She didn't probe. I still had an I.V. in my arm, and something was still dripping into my body out of a bottle hung on a pole. By now, however, I had learned to handle my own post-bowel movement exercises, even while attached to a pole. Dedra, I am certain, remains eternally thankful for that.

My legs and feet ached. I was told that was because of the bypass surgery. Those two big veins had been taken out of my legs, and I wasn't getting the normal blood supply to those extremities. The top of my right foot was incredibly tender to the touch. It still was three months after the surgery when I was also still wrapping each foot in Ace bandages.

I hate to keep going back to my bowels, but it's necessary to explain how I got back into Emory.

I did a short number two one day at home. I did another short number two, and then another and another.

I'm still having some problems with the hemorrhoids, and now I've got diarrhea. Then I noticed the blood.

I decided it was the hemorrhoids and not to tell anybody. It would stop.

It didn't stop. I bled each time I went to the bathroom all one day and into the night. The next morning, it happened again.

I said to Dedra, "I think I have a problem."

I told her I was bleeding with my bowel movements. We were in the Emory emergency room in half an hour.

"This isn't good," is what I could read in Dr. Martin's face. He's bleeding again. Another infection? I was already taking the blood-thinner medication for the new valve. Break out the experimental drugs again.

I mentioned earlier that doctors are thorough. Dr. Martin said, "I want to call a G.I. man to look at you."

If you ever hear the term "G.I. man," run for it. A G.I. man is a doctor that deals with the gastric system, including the intestines.

Oh, hell. Why do on with this charade? He's a butt doctor. That's what I said. *A butt doctor.* He doctors people's butts, which means he makes a living sticking things up you-know-where.

I always wondered: Now here you are out of medical school. You have several choices. You could be a heart doctor, a brain doctor, an ear, nose, and throat doctor, a foot or hand doctor, and yet you decide to spend your entire career sticking things up people's butts.

The butt doctor came in. It wasn't thirty seconds until he had his finger up my butt. He wasn't completely satisfied, however, so he went and got the *head* butt doctor.

He didn't stick his finger in my butt, but he said he thought he ought to do this test on me. He named the test, which I'd never heard of before, but I knew enough to ask, "Will this involve sticking anything in my butt?"

"But of course," said the head butt doctor.

Was that a hint of a smile?

So they kept me overnight. The next morning, they took me up to G.I. to do what the chronology describes—on April 26—as a "limited colonoscopy (50 cm) to splenic flexure after sigmoidoscopy."

I now recall when the HBD named the test, I had thought I had heard the term "flexible," which was somewhat reassuring. When they are talking about ramming something up your butt, the term "flexible" is always preferable to "rigid."

The lady in charge of me in G.I. said she read my columns and was a big fan. She said she was going to give me something to relax me.

"How much should I give him?" she asked Dr. Martin.

"Just a small dose," he said. "This isn't that bad a procedure. I've had it done myself."

As Dr. Martin had explained it to me, the head butt doctor would insert a small tube (half the size of a garden hose, I figured) into my rectum, and he would go up just a short ways, and it would be a "piece of cake."

"Please don't speak of food at a time like this," I said to him.

I was told to turn over on my side. I'm not certain how they did it, but there was an image on the screen of my colon all of a sudden. I distinctly remember a nurse saying, "What pretty pink tissue."

I wasn't sure how to react to this. Was that a compliment? I had never had anybody say of my colon before, "What pretty pink tissue," but I supposed it was better than "What a godawful mess."

And she had made the statement to a man suffering from hemorrhoids, diarrhea, and some sort of gastric bleeding, doctors believed.

The procedure was under way. It really wasn't that bad. I was quite comfortable. There was really no discomfort. There was not a single worrisome murmur out of any of the medical personnel in the room.

Then something happened. I'm not certain how to describe it. All I know is I was just lying there, thinking how this was a piece of cake after all, when something exploded inside my stomach. The pain was incredible. Nothing like I had ever felt before.

I came a foot off the bed and grabbed the railing and began to scream out every curse word I could think of, including one that starts with F. Dr. Martin said later I used it as a noun, verb, and even dangled it as a participle a time or two.

Here's what had happened: Mr. Smarty Britches head butt doctor had gone to the point he was supposed to go up my butt ("limited" colonscopy), couldn't find anything, and decided to go all the way. In order to do that, he had to pump air into me to dilate my intestines. That, I learned, was what hurt so badly.

They had a time with me after that. I'm not certain what-all I said to the physical-therapy nurse, but I can't believe it was half as bad as what I said to all those around me after the air shot.

Dr. Martin pleaded ignorance.

"I didn't know he was going to do that," he said.

"Well, why didn't you stop the S.O.B.?" I demanded.

"This isn't my floor," he replied.

What I said to the head butt doctor is, "I'm just glad I wasn't your dog when you were growing up. I'll bet you had something stuck up the poor thing's butt the whole time."

The head butt doctor didn't like me very much. The feeling was mutual. I got my pretty pink tissue and got the hell back down to cardiac where I belonged.

Later that afternoon, I got the old barium treatment. There are two sorts of barium treatments. There is one where you swallow the barium, and the doctors watch it on a screen to see if it flows down through your innards without hitting a blockage.

The other is where they shoot the barium into you with an enema.

Nobody dared mention the word "enema" to me after the Chinese air torture. So I swallowed all this barium, and it was awful-tasting. At one point, a new doctor walked into the room, a spiffy sort, wearing a Rolex, an Armani suit, and a pair of Gucci suedes. I didn't like his manner. He was very bossy.

He shoved a small cup at me.

"Put this in your mouth," he demanded. "Then I'll give you some water, and you are to swallow."

As soon as I put whatever it was in the cup into my mouth, it began to react with the saliva in my mouth. It was sort of like it felt when I used to try to eat Kool-Aid.

The doctor handed me another cup with a small amount of water in it. As soon as that water hit that stuff in my mouth, that stuff went everywhere, but mainly in two places—on the doctor's Rolex and on his Gucci suedes. He left in a huff.

"It could have been worse!" I hollered to him as he disappeared out of the room.

The butt doctor couldn't find a problem, and the barium didn't show anything, either, and the bleeding stopped the next morning, and I went back home. They finally decided it had been the hemorrhoids.

It was six weeks after the surgery. I was getting around a lot better. I was able to get a bit more comfortable in the bed, so my sleep improved. My appetite was returning. I was still around a strapping 148, but at least I could eat something besides grapes. Sweet Dedra toiled away in the kitchen, even trying to learn certain Southern delicacies like country-fried steak, not easy for a former homecoming queen formerly married to an Italian guy who did all the cooking.

My legs and feet still ached. But I was home with cable, so I didn't have to watch Donahue or Geraldo any more. They were probably interviewing people who ate boogers.

I suppose taking a shower was my biggest problem. Getting into the shower and getting out wasn't the problem. It's just that when somebody opens your chest, your chest remains tender for a long time, and the last thing you want is a steady bead of water pounding down on it. After my first two surgeries, I could always tell when I was completely over all the side effects—when I would turn and allow the water to cascade over my chest in the shower. That was usually about four months out.

So I would always shower with my back to the nozzle. I was still stiff, so it wasn't that easy to lift my arms and shampoo my hair, but I managed to get it done. I didn't bother to try to bend over and wash my feet. I figured the water was hitting them anyway and getting that done.

Still, it was a pain to shower. I took one only when Dedra would absolutely insist, as in, "Good God, you smell worse than Catfish."

It was after a shower one morning, though, that I took a giant step during my recovering period.

I decided it was time to take a long look at my naked body. I was afraid to do this before. I knew they had chopped me up pretty good, but I wasn't exactly sure where-all I would find scars. I was amazed after my first two surgeries how the scars down the middle of my chest eventually healed and nearly disappeared.

Very little of the hair had grown back on my chest after Dedra had shaved it off in the hospital before surgery, so I would be able to see every little nick.

I got out of the shower and toweled off. I stood in front of the mirror naked. I gave myself a long perusal.

Let me put it to you this way: I looked like I'd been in an ax fight and had finished fifth. Remember when they cut up Joe Don Baker playing Sheriff Buford Pusser in the first, and only good, *Walking Tall*, and he took off his shirt in the courtroom to show the astonished and horrified audience?

I looked worse than that. I had the slice down the middle, of course, but then I had scars left and right and up and down. I had big, nasty scars and little pesky ones. I had long scars and short scars. I had a scar down where I still had a pacemaker, and the pacemaker, still in me (they said I'll probably need it sooner or later) was jutting out of the left side of my belly. I had scars that were beginning to heal, but I also had scars that still had scabs on them and were terribly painful to the touch and hurt when I tried to stretch certain parts of my body.

But I found only one scar that really surprised me. I found a big ugly scar deep into my groin area.

"What the hell is this?" I wondered.

Then I thought to myself, I'm getting old. I'll be forty-seven soon, and then fifty before I know it. I wonder if, as a courtesy, they might have slipped in one of those penile implants for when the zip is completely gone off the fastball.

You've heard about those things. You have a little pump somewhere, and when you need to, you hit the pump and up comes your Johnson and stays that way until you pump it back down.

I got fairly excited. Here was a scar I could learn to live with.

But I couldn't find the pump. On my next visit, I asked Dr. Martin about that scar. He said it was for one of those roller pumps. Damn.

I also noticed that what little butt I had was gone. I was born with little or no butt. I don't know if that had something to do with possibly being conceived on a train, too, but I do know that throughout my entire life people have seen me and said one of two things about my butt:

—"Your pants look like a family of Mexicans just moved out of the seat."

—Or, "Good God, Lewis! They've stolen your butt!"

You've seen men with butts like mine. They just don't have one. I don't care how tight a pair of jeans I buy, you couldn't make out a butt on me with a magnifying glass. Snow-skiing pants didn't even fit snugly on my bottom back when I was still crazy and went two thousand miles to be cold and miserable in snow.

Well, from looking in that mirror, I could see that I *really* didn't have a butt anymore.

I phoned Dr. Martin.

"Say," I began, "you guys didn't take what was left of my butt in O.R. Four did, you?"

As the weeks passed, I came along and came along. When I felt strong enough, I moved to a home I have on Lake Okonee, eighty miles east of Atlanta. I'm directly across the lake from the eighteenth hole of the Great Waters Golf Course, a brilliant Jack Nicklaus-designed course with ten of the last eleven holes on the water. They gave me a golf cart up at the clubhouse, and I even started doing some chipping and putting at the practice green.

My appetite improved incredibly. The Lake Okonee area is blessed with country eateries. I wallowed in the food. I had all the fried chicken and country-fried steak and pork chops I wanted, along with fresh vegetables, including fried green tomatoes. I ate so many fried green tomatoes that when I looked into the towel rack, I began to see Fannie Flagg, who wrote the book from which the movie was made.

Two months out of surgery, I started writing my column again. In one, I wrote about all the good things I was getting to eat at Lake Okonee. This started a flood of phone calls both to the newspaper and to Emory.

People wanted to know how I could be eating all that grease after my heart attack.

I hadn't had a heart attack. My diet was not the problem. Dr. Martin had said. "Eat whatever you want. Just gain some weight."

I started gaining weight. I was back to 160 three months out of surgery.

It wasn't always pleasant around me. I wasn't always nice to Dedra. Or Jordan. Or Steve. Or James. Or Catfish.

"Depression is normal," they told Dedra.

Didn't make it any easier. I need to get her a T-shirt that says, "I survived Lewis Grizzard's third heart surgery."

Survival.

There is that word again.

How did I manage it?

It was the skill of the doctors, of course. It was the skill and the great care of all the medical personnel involved in my case. It had to do with the wonderful technology of today. Oh, the magic they can weave in medicine.

They raised me back from near-dead. I was a gone goose. My heart wouldn't beat, for crying out loud. I had thirty hours' worth of operations in thirty six. The only way I stayed alive after that was because somebody once invented the heart-lung machine.

And when I had come off that thing, Dr. Mark Connelly of the transplant team at Emory suggested those roller pumps, and I held on with those somehow.

I nearly bled to death, what was it, three times? There were those experimental drugs again.

Because I was out of it the whole time, I would have given all the credit to the doctors if nobody had told me any differently after the crisis.

They came to my bedside and said things I never thought I would hear such people of science say.

One said, "A higher power was looking after you. I still don't know how you made it."

Another said, "I now believe in miracles."

Dr. Randolph Martin said, "My friend, if you don't believe in the power of prayer now, you never will. I certainly do."

Of course. I remembered then. In the last column before I entered Emory, I had asked readers to pray for me.

But does anybody take anything like that seriously in 1993?

They do. Yes, indeed, they do.

✱✱✱ 9 ✱✱✱

THEY SAID THEY'D NEVER SEEN ANYTHING LIKE IT AT Emory. The switchboard, they told me, never stopped raging during my most critical times. And the messages were always the same:

"Tell Lewis we're praying for him."

My newspaper syndicate, the Atlanta papers, and the hospital received fifty thousand pieces of mail.

"Get well," the cards said. "We're praying for you."

When the news broke that I was on the transplant list, somebody said the hospital got a call from a convent in Kentucky. A nun was dying of a brain tumor. The sisters offered me the dying nun's heart.

A man is said to have called and offered his own heart.

"I don't have anything left to live for," he is said to have said. "Maybe Lewis does."

Every day I have been out in public since my surgery, somebody has come up to me and said something like, "Glad to see you're doing better. My Sunday school class really prayed hard for you."

A man wrote, "My prayer group met at my house, and we did nothing for two hours but pray for you."

That has not stopped since I was out of the hospital.

Over at Lake Okonee, I was having dinner at a local restaurant. An older man came to my table, took my hand, and said, "Young man, we're sure glad you're still with us. My wife and I never gave up on you or stopped praying for you. As long as there is somebody to pray, there is a chance things will work out. Don't ever forget that."

There were tears in the old man's eyes as he walked away from me. There were tears in mine, too.

An entire family drove all the way from Louisiana to be at Emory to pray for me.

Reverend Gilbert Steadham, whom I asked Dedra to get to pray at my funeral, was with me and the family at Emory. I know he must have kept the prayer lines busy.

I even heard that former Atlanta mayor Andy Young said he prayed for me. And I try not to be very nice to politicians in my column.

Once I became aware of the efforts and the

prayers of all who were involved, I began to wonder—how on earth will I ever let these people know how much I appreciate it? They had to have had something to do with the fact that I was still alive. Too many medical folk had said it wasn't all their work.

First, I am trying to answer each card, each letter, with a simple "Thank you." The *Atlanta Journal and Constitution* and King Features Syndicate are helping with that at this writing. I am grateful to them, too.

Second, I decided I would try to get a permit to hold a large meeting in the parking lot at Atlanta Stadium. What I was going to do was invite everybody who prayed for me to come. Then, one by one, I was going to hug their blessed necks and say, "From the very bottom of my heart, I want you to know I couldn't have made it without you."

I couldn't get a permit. Politicians.

So, what I did after that was write my first return column as a thank-you note. I hope a lot of people read it and know just how I feel. And maybe I can say it even better here:

For a long time, I will be asked this question: "So, how are you feeling these days?"

And it's an easy answer now.

I just say, "Loved. I'm really feeling loved."

☞ ♥ ☜

I suppose I should point out, however, that since I have been writing in the paper again, not all my correspondence or that to the papers has been positive. I wrote something a Georgia Tech fan didn't like, and he wrote me, saying, "I prayed for you to live, but I wished I hadn't."

I also got a letter that said, "I prayed for you when you were dying because I was afraid if you died, you would go to hell."

Then there was the liberal boob who wrote the *Constitution* editorial page and said, "Prayer isn't what saved Lewis Grizzard. He is a wealthy man who could afford the very best in medical care. Not every American can, but if we will listen to Hillary Clinton . . ."

Give that man a limbaughsectomy.

☞ ♥ ☜

There is one other thing. How many times has it been said to me, "God has something left for you to do, or he wouldn't have spared you"?

Or, "God doesn't hand over miracles that easily. Take care of the one he gave you"?

Or, "You've got a second chance. Don't blow it"?

To be honest, I've been feeling some pressure about this. There seems to be an awesome responsibility here. After being given this miraculous reprieve, how, then, to deal with it?

Will I be more religious?

If my Methodist Lord hadn't been listening, all those prayers wouldn't have mattered. I know that for a fact. A fact. I'm now looking for a church that still sings the old songs.

Am I thankful to still be alive?

I'll be looking down on Sanford Stadium grass

this football season instead of being spread on top of it. You bet I'm thankful.

Will you change your lifestyle, Lewis?

One side of me says to answer that, "Not only no, but hell, no." That's because I am so sick of the Lifestyle Police, the Cigarette Patrol, and the Whiskey Nazis.

What's going on in this country? They'll be shooting smokers on the streets before it's over. In seven thousand restaurants in Los Angeles, you can't smoke anymore. Half the people in this country think we ought to legalize cocaine so we can get tax money for it. Half those people also would be for gouging out the eyes of smokers.

If somebody doesn't want you to smoke in his house, that's certainly his right. But I was watching television, and some do-gooder wanted people with children to stop smoking in their *own* houses because of secondhand smoke. And it won't be long before some kid sues his parents because they smoked when he or she was growing up.

I don't want to make anybody else uncomfortable. I don't want to give anybody else cancer. But enough is enough here.

And the booze. My reputation as a drinker far outstretched my actual drinking. I couldn't stay awake long enough to drink as much as I once did.

But, "There are more old drunks than there are old doctors," Willie Nelson once sang.

I'll tell you where the country is with drinking these days. The United States Open golf champion this year was wearing a shirt and a hat plugging nonalcoholic beer.

You smoke, you die. You drink, you die. You eat all that greasy food, you die. You don't jog, you don't aerobicize, you die.

So one night you're sitting in your living room reading *Health and Prevention* magazine, and radon gas comes in, goes right up your butt, and kills you. Ha!

I didn't have a heart attack! I don't have a heart condition because of what I smoke, drink, or eat!

I am not about to say that what I put in my body has nothing whatsoever to do with my health, but I suddenly am surrounded by a world of health experts, and it gets tiresome.

"You're eating a greasy cheeseburger, a man in your condition!"

Deliver me.

We'd all be a lot happier if we lived our own lives and allowed the son of a bitch down the street to live his. I just can't put it any more simply or directly than that.

I'm still eating whatever I want, and onions still give me indigestion.

I'm trying to get off the cigarettes. It isn't easy.

I have not had one single ounce of vodka since March 21, 1993.

So there.

Rather than deal with what I am going to *deprive* myself of for whatever time God has been so kind to offer me as an extension on my life, I have been trying to focus on what I am going to *allow* myself to have.

I've worked hard during my life. I'm going to say that about myself. I'm not bragging, by any means. I shouldn't have worked as hard as I have. But I was ambitious. It cost me as much, or more, as it gained me. That pretty blonde I married when I was nineteen might have been my wife for twenty-seven years on July 17, 1993, had I not been so ambitious. I lost a second wife in Chicago because I worked seven days a week at that damn newspaper. I might still be with my third if I had been able to say no when somebody wanted to pay to hear me tell funny stories.

I would like to accomplish the following during my remaining years, in no particular order:

- Goof off more.
- Figure out a way to have more than six months in which to write a book.
- Get my golf handicap down to single digits.
- Attend more movies in the afternoon.
- Stay out of New York City. Stay out of most major cities.
- Cut down by at least half the number of airplanes in which I must ride.
- Stand in a clear stream in a cool place just once and catch a trout on a fly rod.
- Go back to Lugano, Switzerland, for two weeks.
- Find a church where they sing out of the old Methodist Cokesbury Hymnal.

- Visit the site of the Normandy invasion and write about how it feels to stand there.
- Get in some sort of vehicle like a Jeep and travel around writing columns about what's doing in small American towns during the summer.
- Run the middle fork of the Salmon River again, in an inflatable one-man kayak, and remember Browny Stephens.
- Avoid meetings with lawyers.
- And accountants.
- Hit anybody in the mouth who mentions the words "limited partnership" to me.
- Get rid of one helluva lot of real estate.
- See Catfish catch one damn squirrel.
- See Georgia win another national football championship.
- Buy a stock that actually goes up.
- Ride more trains.
- Not give a damn when some millionaire outfielder in an Atlanta Braves uniform misses the cutoff man.
- See a Republican back in the White House.
- Plant a garden and actually harvest my own homegrown tomatoes.
- Never wear another tuxedo.
- Never do six shows in six towns in six nights.
- Write more music with Dick Feller. (We actually got a check—a small one—because a couple of radio stations played "Grandma Willie's Yard," one of ours.)
- Write a funny novel. Any kind of novel, just to prove to myself I could do it.

- Write a book about male friendship.
- Spend August at the Greenbriar in West Virginia.
- Linger over Friday's beef tips and rice at Atlanta's Luckie Street Grill a little longer.
- Find a woman who would cook me fried corned beef that comes in a can and not call it Spam.
- Never experience a fourth divorce.
- Sleep without dreams.
- Put up a basketball backboard in my yard and shoot some hoops when I'm not playing golf.
- Call people I love more often.
- See Rock City. I've never seen the son of a bitch. Honest.
- Avoid having any more heart surgery anytime soon.

And one more thing I would like to accomplish. I would like to make Helen Elliott proud. Helen published my first six books. People often ask me, "How do I get a book published?"

It's not easy. How I did it was first get turned down. I got a letter from an editor, who was from the South, at Doubleday in New York. He said a friend in Atlanta had written him and had said he liked my columns and thought Doubleday might be interested in a collection.

I sent the man some columns. He wrote back and said, "Sorry."

I happened to mention that one night to a friend who had once worked for a publisher in New York and knew of this lady, Helen Elliott, who had just started Peachtree Publishers in Atlanta.

So I met with Helen. She gave me an advance of five hundred dollars, published my first book, *Kathy Sue Loudermilk, I Love You*, and would do five more.

Helen Elliott was an angel herself. No sweeter, kinder woman have I ever met. She would say to me often, "One day, I hope you'll write my story."

For now, the short version:

Helen was the daughter of a former radio hell-and-brimfire preacher in Augusta, Georgia. When she was sixteen, her father enrolled her in Bob Jones University in Greenville, South Carolina, a believe-it-or-else fundamentalist Christian school.

Even under those strictest of circumstances, Helen, away from her father for the first time, began to waver from her walk-the-line raisings. Then she met a boy named Leonard Elliott, and they fell in love. Helen's father ranted against his daughter even dating, quoting Scripture, naturally; and the idea she, at the tender age of sixteen, might be in danger of falling victim to the evils that lurk in young men caused him to forbid the relationship to continue.

Helen and Leonard eloped. It would be nearly forty years before she next spoke to her father.

Helen told me she wrote off religion after that. She had children, and she and Leonard raised a family and supported themselves in the music-publishing business. Helen often spoke to her husband about starting a book-publishing company, too. Freed to read whatever she pleased, she had developed a love and vast respect for the free release of ideas.

But it just never happened.

Until a doctor told Helen, at age fifty-five, that she had cancer.

"The prognosis wasn't good," Helen would tell me. "I think they were telling me it was over. The cancer wasn't in the early stages. I came back from the doctor's office that day figuring I would have to measure my life in terms of months and weeks. That night, I did something I never thought I would do again—I prayed and asked the Lord to forgive me for turning against Him. I also asked Him for something else.

"I prayed, 'God, give me five more years. Give me five more years, and I'm going to start a book-publishing company.' "

Helen's cancer went into remission. The publishing company was a great success. She and her father were reunited. And our lives crossed.

I sought the help of many to get me through my first surgery. I talked to ministers, old guitar players, poets, close friends, members of my family, and, naturally, my wife.

But Helen helped me most. She said:

"To do this and to get through it will be like going to the moon and back. You will never be the same, and you will grow from it. These last years of my life have been the very best of my life, and had I not had my own health crisis, I would never have fulfilled this dream of publishing books."

Then she smiled and said, "Everything's going to be all right."

She was standing in for my invalid mother.

Helen's cancer came back after she had built her publishing company into a very successful one. She lived five more years after her prayer.

If I can accomplish half in my allotted time of what Helen did in her five years, I think she would look down at me and say, "You did fine."

And, Helen, I've been to Mars and back this time, but I'm still able to laugh.

Dr. Henry Langhorne of Emory told me this story:

"We had a guy in here from up in the hills of North Georgia. We had to replace both his mitral and aortic valves with mechanicals like you have now.

"He had to take the blood thinner like you do. You have to take it every day for the rest of your life.

"Well, he did fine, and we sent him home. Later, however, he came back in an awful shape. He was all clogged up in there, and he was shooting off clots. He was in really bad shape, and we had to replace both valves again.

"He finally admitted to us he had stopped taking his blood thinner. And guess why? He was a big poker player. But after his operation, he started losing all the time, and he just couldn't figure it out.

"But he finally did. As I'm sure you've noticed [I have], that valve makes a clicking noise sometimes. And the harder your heart beats, the louder the tick. So every time this guy would get a great hand, his heart would start beating harder. The other players could hear the ticks, know he was loaded, and they would fold. He couldn't beat anybody."

"But he started taking the blood thinner again after that?"

"Yeah," said Dr. Langhorne. "I guess he figured life was more valuable than any poker pot."

Life.

I do love that word.

✳✳✳ Epilogue ✳✳✳

Last summer, I was invited to go fishing in Western British Columbia for a taping of the ESPN program *Suzuki's Great Outdoors with Dick Butkus*. I was in Orlando on business. I flew from Orlando to Salt Lake City to Portland to Vancouver to Campbell River, B.C., and then I took a ferry to Quadra Island, B.C.

I left Orlando in the early morning. I had to change planes in Portland.

The flight from Portland to Vancouver left at 11:11 Pacific Daylight Time.

We made it.

☞ ♥ ☜

I still have the end of my finger.

LEWIS GRIZZARD

Published by Ballantine Books.
Available in your local bookstore.